The Magic of Crazy Quilting

A Complete Resource For Embellished Quilting

J. Marsha Michler

krause publications

700 East State St., Iola, WI 54990-0001
Telephone 715-445-2214
www.krause.com

Photography by J. Marsha Michler (unless otherwise stated)
Illustrations by J. Marsha Michler
Book design by Jan Wojtech

Library of Congress Cataloging-in-Publication Data
   Michler, J. Marsha
   The Magic of Crazy Quilting/ J. Marsha Michler
   144   cm.
   Includes index, bibliography, resources.
   ISBN 0-87341-622-8
       1. Quilting   2. Needlework   3. Crazy Quilt
       Documentation/History
       I. Michler, J. Marsha II. Title.
       CIP 98-84098

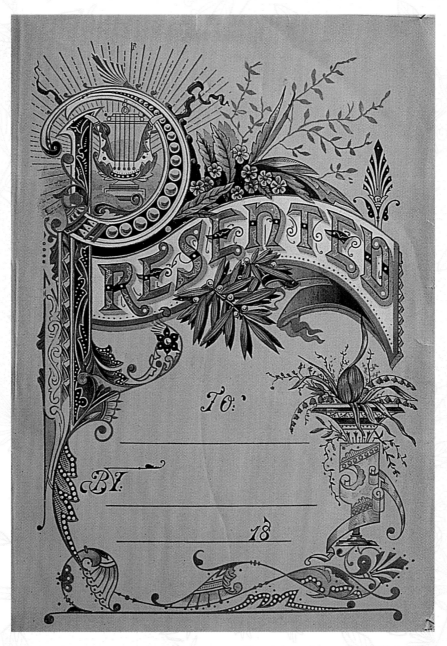

Frontpiece from an 1800's book.

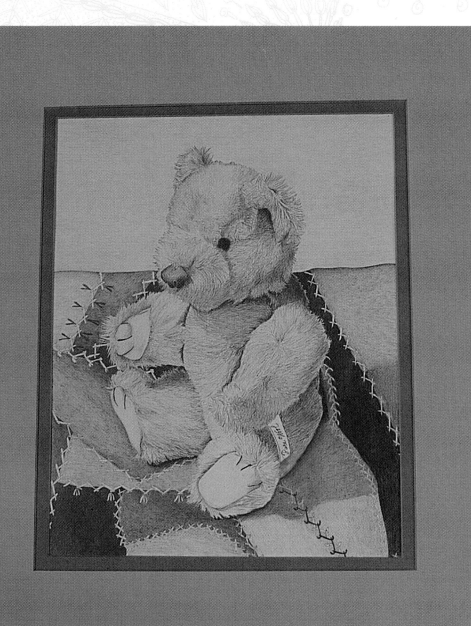

Teddy bear on a crazy quilt. Pencil drawing by the author.

For their loving patience and understanding
while this project came together,
I dedicate this book to my son Ben and to Paul.
I could not have done it without you.

Acknowledgments

My most heartfelt thanks to all of those who contributed in so many ways to this book. Thanks to all the wonderful people at Krause including my editors, Gabrielle Wyant-Perillo and Kris Manty, and book designer Jan Wojtech; my agent, Sandy Taylor for believing in me; Joe Hudgins, who generously shared his knowledge of cigarette silks; Diana Vandervoort for her gracious encouragement; Cindy Smith, **Limerick Public Library**, for her research assistance; Paula Robert of **Copy-It**, Biddeford, Maine; Jeannette Brewster, President of **Valley Needlers Quilt Guild**.

Many thanks to those who generously contributed supplies, photographs and other materials: Kim Kovaly, **The Willow Shop**; Maggie Backman, **Things Japanese**; Anna Baird, **Green Mountain Hand Dyed Linens**; Nancy Kirk, **The Kirk Collection**; Dena Lenham, Design Coordinator of **Kreinik Mfg. Co., Inc.**; Elda O'Connell, Catherine Carpenter; Mary Weinberg.

My deepest thanks to the following businesses, institutions, and people for kindly and generously allowing access to crazy quilts for study and photography:

Betsey Telford, owner of **Rocky Mountain Quilts**
130 York St.
York Village, ME 03909

Richard T. Eisenhour, Curator of Collections
Marcene J. Modeland, Director
Pamela S. Eagleson, Acting Director
The Brick Store Museum
117 Main St.
Kennebunk, ME 04043

Joan Sylvester, owner of **Shiretown Antique Center**
Rt. 202
Alfred, ME 04002

Bonnie Hayward, owner of **Avalon Antiques**
on display at Arundel Antiques
1713 Portland Rd.
Arundel, ME 04046

The Gold Bug Antiques
U.S. Rt. 1
Cape Neddick, ME
http://www.antiques4you.com/~victique/

The Barn at Cape Neddick
U.S. Rt. 1
Cape Neddick, ME 03902

Tina Toomey, **Curator of York Institute Museum**
371 Main St.
Saco, ME 04072

Maine Historical Society
485 Congress St.
Portland, ME 04101

Thanks to **Dover Publications, Inc**. for permission to use Victorian clip art from its "Pictorial Archives.":
Victorian Frames, Borders and Cuts, from the **1882 Type Catalog of George Bruce's Son and Co.,** 1976,
Grafton, Carol Belanger, ed., **Victorian Pictorial Borders**, 1984,
Derriey, Charles, **Borders, Frames and Decorative Motifs from the 1862 Derriey Typographic Catalog**, 1987,
Grafton, Carol Belanger, ed., **Treasury of Victorian Printers' Frames, Ornaments and Initials**, 1984,
Grafton, Carol Belanger, **Victorian Spot Illustrations, Alphabets and Ornaments, from Porret's Type Catalog**, 1982.

Also, my thanks, deepest appreciation and admiration to Limerick's very special "quilters," who are: Kim and Lauren Kovaly, Marian Budzyna, Jane Bryant, Kathy Melzer, Adele and Ruth Floyd, Paul Baresel and Peg Gomane.

Contents

Introduction

The years marked by Queen Victoria's reign, 1838-1901, were characterized by massive and significant social changes. The romance in this age is in the phenomenal opening of trade, the boom in technology and the creation of entrepreneurialism. The "Iron Horse" began to course its way across entire continents. Toilets became flushable, silks became available and affordable and telegraph cables literally connected continents. Electricity created easy lighting of a home and medical discoveries found new ways to save lives. The color mauve was discovered, the sewing machine was invented and the search was on for a synthetic silk.

With industry, art was undergoing major changes. Painters studied the science of light and color. They began juxtaposing colors in ways that the eye would mix them. Artists such as Monet sought to capture the effects of light, while Seurat created paintings entirely of dots. These and other artists were the vanguardists of the modern art movement. They were very different from the prior academic style, of realistically rendering subjects, with layer upon layer of well-oiled paint.

A showpiece antique crazy quilt. Collection of, and photographed at Rocky Mountain Quilts, York Village, Maine.

Victorian-age needlework was rich and varied. It is fitting that women in their quilting, reacting to the changes around them, attempted unconventional forms. The play of colors and textures placed on a quilt top, and united with embroidery stitches, are every bit as artistic as the works of the painters. Some crazy quilts of late Victorian times display a range of highly developed needlework skills, combined with a refined sense of color and composition. These quilts often feature ribbonwork, ribbon embroidery, monogramming, embroidery stitches of all types and other forms of needlework. At times, they included paintings on fabric; a complex mix of ingredients.

There is no identifiable "inventor" of the crazy quilt. It seems to have been congruous with the era in which it was born. Similar to the fads that occur today, crazy quilting took off of its own volition. It appears to have originated in America and gained steam from about 1860. The phase culminated around the 1880s and fizzled out in the early 1900s. The appeal of crazy quilting to Victorian ladies must have subsequently inspired the rage. These ladies would have adored the same we do today–that of seeking out a wonderful collection of "finds," fancy fabrics and luxurious threads. These valuables are then assembled into a showpiece quilt.

About Crazy Quilting

Crazy quilting is the placing together of irregular-shaped patches, usually onto a foundation, after which they are usually secured with embroidery stitches. Often used are fancy fabrics from dressmaking, draperies, bridal apparel and other sources. A wide variety of embellishments and embroidery stitches, added to the patches, dramatically bring the patched surface to life. The true magic of crazy quilting is in the melding of its ingredients and the individuality of each hand's work. There is a magical transformation that takes place with the laying of patches and the addition of embroidery stitches and embellishments. You never truly know what it is going to look like until the final stitches are placed.

The word "crazy" beautifully sums up what is unique about this type of quilt. It is perfect if you feel a little bit crazy while working on one! This form of quilting utilizes your most pure imaginativeness from beginning to end. For those who make these quilts, the joy of creativity will truly blossom.

How to Use This Book

Read this book from front to back or use it as a reference volume. I recommend that beginners read it through to become familiar with the basic procedures and the many options. More experienced workers may prefer to reference individual topics.

I present **The Magic of Crazy Quilting** with the crazy quilt in mind. However, the techniques on the pages apply to a variety of quilt types and many needlework projects.

PART ONE
The Basics of Crazy Quilting

A treadle and an early Singer are still dependable workhorses today. A basket of silks awaits a new project. The wall-hanging quilt is available as a pattern. (See sources).

Simple Requirements

There are a few essential tools for crazy quilting. If you have done sewing or traditional quilting, there is a good chance they are already part of your repertoire. Essential tools include shears, pins, iron and ironing board, tape measure, cutting mat, and a basic sewing machine. For embroidery, you will need embroidery scissors, needles, pincushion and a hoop. Additional requirements for different types of embroidery and embellishments are covered in Artful Embellishments.

Purchase quality tools and you will find that, with proper care, they will last a lifetime. Quality tools are an excellent investment and make a difference in your level of sewing enjoyment.

Shears and Scissors

The shears I use for patch cutting are 7 inches long, slightly shorter than the standard 8-inch shears. A good shears is very sharp and cuts fabric so easily that cutting is effortless. Mine is all metal, and the blades can be honed to keep them sharp.

There are many different styles and sizes of embroidery scissors. My favorite is a multi-functional 5-inch metal knife-edge scissors with both a narrow and a wide blade. The narrow blade is needle-sharp for picking out unwanted stitches. When trimming thread ends and fabrics on a patched quilt top, place the wide blade next to the fabric. For safety and to protect the

blades when not in use, store the scissors in a sheath or other holder. Purchase a ceramic hone to retain the cutting edges of knife-edge scissors. Be sure to follow the manufacturer instructions.

Add a paper-cutting scissors to your tool collection. Use this to cut out paper patterns and tissue paper. Do not use a fabric shears or embroidery scissors to cut paper, as this horrendously dulls the blades.

A good scissors to treasure,
Is both delight and pleasure.
But in public is not to share -
Too likely to dis-a-pair!

Only a few tools are required for crazy quilting. Some antique tools are still viable today, such as the pincushion/thread stand here.

When traveling with a project, take along an inexpensive thread clippers instead of your good embroidery scissors. Like pens, scissors are often borrowed or they can unknowingly fall out of your bag. Also, a sharp-pointed scissors presents safety concerns.

Needles and Pins

Three types of hand-sewing needles will accommodate almost any technique in crazy quilting: embroidery/crewel, chenille and applique/size 12 sharps.

For use with a variety of threads and ribbons, purchase assortments of the embroidery and chenille needles. Needles vary in quality. My favorites, manufactured by Piecemakers®, slide effortlessly through fabric and have smooth eyes.

The purpose of the needle is to make a hole in the fabric that is large enough to easily allow a thread or embroidery ribbon to pass. At the same time, it should hold the thread snug enough to prevent slipping out of the eye.

Although they slip through and stick fingers, evade grasp and often become stuck in the carpet, pins are among the most useful of tools. Having discovered silk pins, I now use them for almost everything. They create little bulge in the fabric and pressing is easier because the heads are smaller. If using pins with beaded heads, choose those with glass beads to prevent melting under the iron.

Embroidery Hoops

An embroidery hoop is essential for handstitching on projects patched onto such lightweight foundations as silk organza and batiste. This also applies to embellishments such as beading and punchneedle. A 3-inch or 4-inch hoop is an excellent size for small, silk ribbon embroideries. Hoops 6 inches or larger are useful for embroidering along patch seams.

I use hoops imported from Germany. These are a smooth wood hoop with a brass screw.

To protect delicate fabrics and prevent hoop marks, wrap the hoop with a strip of clean batiste or another soft fabric. When you set a project aside, always remove the hoop.

Projects worked on a muslin foundation, and patched with firm fabrics, such as satins, velveteen and cottons, do not always require a hoop for embroidery. Try embroidering without a hoop to determine if the piece will stay smooth. Use a hoop if it tends to bunch.

One of my favorite tools is the supported lap hoop. This is a quilting hoop, raised above a base, on supports of wood or metal. Both hands remain free for stitching and doing embellishment work because the hoop rests on your lap or a table. I use a 14-inch round lap hoop, particularly for punchneedle, beading and embroidering silk quilts.

A lap hoop is easily portable. The only drawback is in fastening the ends of embroidery and beading threads. It is a bit clumsy to fasten the ends on the back of the work. Instead of turning the hoop over, secure and conceal ends on the front by making several tiny stitches beneath the edge of a patch or an embellishment.

Laying Tool

Use a laying tool, for embroideries such as Oriental, satin stitch, monogramming, silk ribbon and needlepoint. When pulling the thread or ribbon through the fabric to the back, run it over the laying tool to remove any excess twist. This specialty tool also allows the thread to lie smoothly on the surface of the fabric. In silk work, this is important for the maximum sheen of the fiber to show. The project must be in a supported hoop, since one hand holds the laying tool and the other hand works the stitches.

Iron and Ironing Board

Essential to all patching methods, careful pressing helps ensure a smooth quilt surface. Press all patched quilt tops and embroideries face down on a padded surface. Use a padded ironing board cover or a terry cloth towel placed over the ironing board.

When patching, use a dry iron to avoid scorching your fingers. When steam is required, use a spray bottle and spray the surface of the ironing board. To prevent water-spotting, do not spray the patch.

Use a press cloth on delicate fabrics and on those that pressing may cause a shiny surface.

A laying tool is held in the left hand, while the needle is used in the right. (Reverse for left-handedness). This tool is used to assist thread or embroidery ribbon to lie smoothly on the surface of the fabric. The quilt top is in a lap, or supported hoop.

TIP: "Pressing" is not the same as "ironing." To press, place the iron on the fabric and lightly press for a few seconds. Be careful not to scorch. I do not recommend sliding the iron around on embroidery, embellishments or patches, as this can move materials out of place.

Sewing Machine

Unless you are going to machine embroider around the crazy-quilt patches, a sewing machine with only a simple, straight stitch setting is necessary. The older, smaller machines called "featherweights" are more than ideal. Even a treadle is acceptable!

The machine manual specifies maintenance, necessary operation information and special purpose instructions.

NOTE: Throughout this book, the words "fabric" or "fabrics" describe cloth.
The word "materials" often denotes fabric yardage. However, in this book materials may also include laces, ribbons, threads and miscellaneous items used in a quilt or a project.

A Workspace

Set up a workspace in an area large enough to place an ironing board next to a table or desk. It is far easier to have a permanent space to work than it is to repeatedly set up and take down. An entire room is, of course, the most ideal situation. If this is not possible, a corner or nook is next best. Space in an attic or a basement can be converted, although if you have a basement studio, be sure to monitor the humidity. Too much moisture can cause your tools to become rusty and fibers to become musty.

Lighting is very important. Achieve proper lighting with good fixtures or a combination of windows and fixtures. In the necessary position, place or position a clamp-on light with an adjustable arm. Fit these, or other types, with ener-

gy-saving fluorescent bulbs. Choose fluorescent or incandescent lighting according to personal preference. For accuracy, I make my color choices in natural daylight. This allows me to work on the project under any type of lighting.

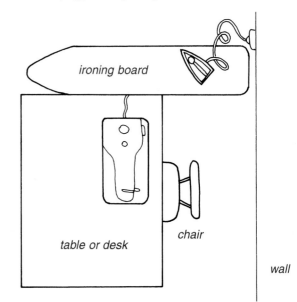

The machine-sewn methods of crazy quilting are easiest with an ironing board placed next to the sewing machine.

For large projects, a table is helpful for hand-patching methods. With an ironing board placed alongside, use a kitchen, dining or fold-up table. Place a large cutting mat on the table to protect it from being scratched by pins and needles.

If you are using a machine method of patching, place the ironing board within reach of the sewing machine. For safety, always set an ironing board and iron against a wall and near an outlet.

A bookcase, or space on a bookshelf, will keep your needlework references handy. Put your magazines or magazine clippings in binders. These materials will inspire project ideas, provide answers, give examples and offer suggestions. In one volume, a good how-to book is equivalent to an entire class or seminar.

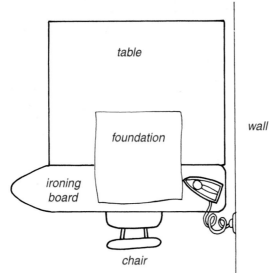

A table placed next to an ironing board is a convenient arrangement for patching a crazy quilt by hand.

Natural Elegance

Crazy quilting is an opportunity par excellence to explore fabrics and colors. Fabric types from Victorian times include silks, cottons, linen and wool. These fabrics were available in a wide variety of textures, weaves and surface finishes. In the late 1800s, in an attempt to imitate silk, it was discovered that rayons and acetate synthetics could be derived of natural materials. Improved in the early 1900s they are invaluable for their beautiful finishes.

The 1800s represented a burgeoning of new fabric weaves, finishes, types and colors. The invention of the jacquard loom came about for making fabrics with woven-in patterning. Experimentation to create a synthetic silk was underway and methods of both printing and photography improved. As William Henry Perkin was trying to make synthetic quinine, he accidentally discovered the color mauve, which in turn caused the invention of Aniline dyes. As they sought scraps for their crazy quilts, Victorian ladies likely drooled over some of these new-fangled fabrics and colors! They began to eschew cotton calicos thinking them "drab." They instead made scrap quilts and crazy quilts out of silks and other fine fabrics.

Involved in the assemblage of a crazy quilt is a combination of textures, finishes and colors. Of these, choosing colors presents a great challenge for many of us. Later in this chapter is some information that may be helpful in selecting fabric colors. Also try the dye experiments in part two of Artful Embellishments. Dyeing is an excellent way to learn about colors.

The "White Rose" quilt, 1862, with its many black and white patches displays a strongly contrasting color scheme softened by touches of color. Photographed at Shiretown Antique Center, Alfred, Maine.

An Overview of Fiber Types

Silk

Amazing, exceptional and unique are a few words with which to describe this fiber. Silk has extremely fine fibers with amazing strength. It is exceptional in its translucency and possesses a uniquely dry, crushy texture. This is a "protein" fiber, made of silkworm cocoons. These cocoons are unraveled into a fine strand many yards long. This strand, called "filament silk," is then plied into threads. In comparison, "spun silks" are carded and spun. The filament silks are capable of the highest sheen, while spun silks tend to be matte or nearly matte in finish.

Habotai, taffeta, jacquard, charmeuse, satin, dupion, noil and velvet are some of the weaves and fabric types in which silk is available. Silk fabrics can be crisp as taffeta, or soft and nearly weightless as lightweight Habotai. Finishes vary from matte to shiny and smooth to coarse, depending on the silk and the weave of the fabric.

Silk in its natural state is highly washable. When washed for the first time, shrinkage can occur and some dyes, especially darker colors, may run. Silk garments and yardage, labeled "dry clean only," may not be colorfast and could shrink. Some surface finishes can change with washing. As with other fabric types, test-wash a small piece before immersing the whole piece. Wash silk in lukewarm water with mild soap.

Iron silks on low heat to prevent scorching. If the fabric is crumpled up and wrinkles have set in, apply steam or mist while ironing. Should static occur, try misting the air with water or set the piece aside until the electricity ceases.

Cotton

Cotton is a seed head that forms on the plant after the flower blooms. I tried growing it in my Maine garden, but cotton requires a longer growing season. The plants flowered, but did not go to seed. The result was no cotton to harvest. If you live in the North and wish to try growing cotton, start the seeds early, indoors. Transplant outdoors after the final frost.

Mercerization, cotton treated with caustic soda, was invented in the mid-1800s. This treatment produces high luster, greater strength and more efficient dye absorption.

Some of the finishes and weaves associated with this fiber include broadcloth, twill, velveteen, gauze and corduroy. Cotton is spun from very fine to heavy and coarse fibers. Fabric types vary from lightweight to heavy and from sheer to opaque. Since the fiber itself is opaque, sheerness is obtained by using extremely fine threads or open weaves.

Cotton fabrics can be washed with agitation in hot or cold water. Some shrinkage in the first washing is normal, as is the loss of some excess dye.

Cotton moiré and chintz have glossy surface finishes which tend to wash-out. These polished surfaces are produced by running the fabric through rollers. Although labeled "dry clean only," I prefer to wash them. Washing produces a natural way to "antique" the finish!

Iron cottons on high heat, but take care to avoid scorching. I find for most crazy quilting purposes, a "wool" setting works well.

TIP: Sateen of 100 percent cotton is a beautiful fabric with a soft sheen and elegant drape. Sateen is often used as borders and backings in antique crazy quilts. Its satin weave creates floats of threads that reflect the light. It is occasionally found, from heirloom sewing sources, in white (consider dyeing it) to dressmaking fabric selections. It heartens me to see it used by known designers in luxury sheets and bedding. I hope this beautiful fabric continues to become more widely available. A high-quality sateen has a luxurious-looking finish and both sides of the fabric are free of pilling or fuzzing.

Linen

Linen fabric comes from the flax plant. A laborious process involves rotting away the non-fibrous parts of the plant, then spinning and weaving the resulting fibers. It is woven into fine handkerchief linens or coarser fabrics and canvas.

Linens often have a distinctive luster, especially when starched and pressed. Because the fiber is firm, bordering on stiffness, it makes an ideal even-weave fabric for cross stitch embroidery. Linen easily accepts dye. Use natural dyes to create a wide range of beautiful, luxurious colors.

Linens, more than other fibers, have survived through time. A long-lasting fiber (Egyptian mummies are wrapped in it), it tends to have a feel of age-old elegance. Linen is highly washable and irons on high heat.

Rayon

First appearing in the late 1800s, rayon is the result of a search for synthetic silk. This early rayon was highly flammable. In 1924, another method of making it was discovered. Rayon consists of cellulose fibers derived from wood or cottonseed.

Rayon fabrics range from the drapey challis types to twills, velvets and other finishes. Rayon is used in combination with silk to create velvet. The drapery fabric bengaline, consists of rayon woven over a cotton core.

Rayon presses easily and holds a crease even with finger-pressing. For this reason, the closely woven types are excellent for appliqué. Although weak when wet, it firms up again when dry. Iron rayon on low heat and use cool temperatures for washing.

Acetate

Acetate, also synthesized of cellulose, is an offshoot of the rayon discovery. Acetate, not used commercially until 1924, is often woven into satin or taffeta. Taffeta is sometimes "calendered," or run through rollers to give it a moiré finish. Acetate satin has high luster and firm drape. The taffeta is crisp and, when rubbed against itself, is noisy.

Although sold as "dry clean only," these fabrics are washable by hand. Moiré and some glossy finishes may partly or completely wash out. I often do this intentionally to cut down on shine or to create an "aged" effect. Because the sheen is created by the weave, satins retain their luster.

Like rayon, press these fabrics on low heat. Acetates retain creases well. Wash in a large basin of cool or cold water. DO NOT WRING or creases may remain, even after pressing.

Wool

Here in Maine, where the weather gets chilly, wool is a favorite fiber. A century ago, there may have been many crazy quilts made of wool. Those I found are mostly bed-size and well worn.

Wool fabrics vary from finely woven challis to heavy types that are used for coats and blankets. Suit-weights and challis make excellent crazy patches. Use the blanket stitch appliqué on blanketing and felted wools to eliminate having to hem their edges. Most patterned wool fabrics are woven in plaids, herringbones and pinstripes. Natural sheep-color browns, grays, tans and off-whites are lovely and useful neutral shades.

Wool holds a crease when steamed and allows sculptural forming by steaming (hats are an example). It has a tendency to felt when it is both wet and subjected to agitation. Shocking with temperature changes when it is wet will surely shrink wool.

Fabrics for Crazy Quilting

Luxury and plain fabrics in a mix of textures and surface finishes. From left are wool, velveteen, bengaline, taffeta, moiré taffeta, rayon/cotton, rayon challis, damask, satin, brocade, velveteen. The folded pieces are Green Mountain Hand natural-dyed linens.

Characteristics of fabrics make some easier to work with than others. These include fabrics that are:

a) woven,
b) firm or "crisp" in texture, and
c) hold a crease when pressed.

Napped fabrics, such as velvets, make beautiful crazy patches. However, while working with them, velvets have a tendency to slip and slide. To keep them in place, carefully pin and baste.

The most useful fabrics are solid colors. Beautifully textured, unprinted fabrics add a great deal to a crazy quilt. Solid fabrics nicely flaunt embroidery and other details.

The following is a list of some of the fabric types that are suitable for crazy patches:

Plush: Velvet
    Cotton Velveteen
    No-wale or fine-wale corduroy

Smooth: Satin
    Taffeta
    Chintz
    Cotton Sateen
    Linen
    Cotton Sheeting
    Quilting cottons

Ribbed: Bengaline
    Corduroy
    Some velvets and
      velveteens

Textured: Jacquard
    Damask
    Moiré
    Silks noil, dupion,
      crepe.
    Brocade
    Twill
    Challis
    All-over laces

Washing Instructions for Washable Fabrics

If you are not sure about the washability of a fabric, first test-wash a small piece. Washing by hand allows you observe if the fabric dulls, bleeds dye or excessively shrinks. I like to prewash fabrics soon after purchase. By doing so, I avoid the question: "Was this prewashed or not?"

When you cut up a piece of clothing to use for crazy patch fabrics, and the label says "dry clean only," this could mean that the *fabric* is washable but the *garment* is not washable. For example, interior paddings and interfacings in tailored suits can shift about or lose their shape.

Test-iron any unfamiliar fabrics. I've had upholstery fabrics shrink to half their size when slightly touched by a warm iron.

I use the following method for all of my crazy quilting fabrics:

❶ Use a large basin for acetates to avoid crinkling. Wash other types in a size in which the fabric fits. Use cool to lukewarm water and mild soap. For all fabrics, especially silks and wools, I suggest using unscented natural shampoo that is found at a natural-food store.

❷ Wash silks, rayons, wools and acetates by soaking. Gently move the fabric in the water to work the soap through the fibers. Do not soak dark and light colors together. Cottons and linens can be vigorously washed.

❸ Rinse by repeatedly changing the water until it is clear. Always use the same temperature to rinse and wash. Rinse cottons and linens under running water. If dyes run, keep rinsing until the water is clear. If the dye continues to run after you re-soap the fabric, it is not colorfast and should instead be dry cleaned.

❹ Do not wring acetate, silk or wool fabrics. Wrap the wet fabric in a towel, roll and gently squeeze. Immediately remove the fabric and hang it over a line to dry. Dry all fabrics out of direct sunlight and away from heat sources.

❺ When the fabric is dry, iron at an appropriate temperature. If necessary, use steam.

Mary's Velvet Dilemma

This tale of woe was sent out to nearly 700 members of *Quiltropolis'* crazy quilt email list. The following is an edited version and is used by permission of the author. Mary wrote this spontaneously, the reason for some of the spellings!

"... I was rummaging around today at a yard sale and got a WONDERFUL beautiful deep blue velvet ... coat with a 'furry' white lining and ivory satin sleeves. WHAT A FIND!!!

"Ran home jumped on the bed with a cup of coffee, the tv clicky dude, and SISSORS! Took me the better part of two hours but FINALLY I had everything whacked up.

"Of course at THIS point I have MY TISSUES because there's little tiny tiny NANNO tiny white 'hairs' EVERYWHRERE ... I'm sneezing ... the Pupper is sneezing .... I run down stairs throw the blue velvet in the washer.

"Took out a HUGH ... KNOT of string and velvet. GRRRRRRRR stand there and untangle.

"Throw in (the dryer) to soften and unwrinkle. Pupper now wants out and the phone rings ... GRAB TISSUES ... *finally* make it back to the dryer open the door and FLUFFFF out FLYS bitty blue fluffles EVERYWHERE .... The inside of the door is solid with blue ... I'm sneezing, the Pupper is sneezing....

"...I've sworn the Pupper to silence or no doggie treats!

"Lesson learned: DON'T cut up velvet ... BEFORE washing!"

-reprinted by permission of Mary Weinberg.

TIP: The nap of velvet and velveteen consists of many short fibers. These fibers are held in place by a woven backing. With cut pieces of these fabrics, use a gentle hand-wash or first machine stitch the edges with a zigzag stitch. A serger will nicely overcast raw edges.

Shopping for Fabrics

The right piece of fabric often inspires an entire project. Buy crazy quilting fabric because you love it. Remember, you don't have to wear it or swath a room. Purchase, and actually use, the most outrageous colors and textures.

Shopping and collecting is as inspiring as diving into a new project. Fabrics are gleaned from a number of sources. Search fabric stores for clothing types, quilt shops for cotton solids, upholstery and drapery fabrics stores and bridal shops. Also seek out factory outlets.

January white sales are good for finding high quality, all-cotton sheets. Sheets are excellent fabrics for borders and backings.

Check out linen departments for damask, allover lace tablecloths and other interesting weaves.

Browse second-hand shops and yard sales for hardly-worn evening and tailored wear, especially those made of natural fibers. Take them apart by ripping out the seams or simply cutting along the seam edges. Search for men's ties, especially silk ones, and carefully rip out the stitching.

Although solids are most useful in crazy quilting, collect some prints. The prints used in the Victorian crazies were usually simple foulards, stripes and somewhat plain-looking florals.

Shopping is greatly simplified if you are willing to dye white or natural-color goods. One yard of white fabric easily becomes two to three dozen different colors. Silks in particular are very easy to dye. When selecting dyes, remember to purchase the correct type for the specific fiber being dyed.

Tips for collecting:

- Buy what you like when you see it. If you go back for it later, it may not be there.
- Save scraps down to the smallest possible

Inspiration for a quilt with an Oriental theme, these fabrics are pieces of worn kimonos, from Katie's Vintage Kimono (see Sources). The designs on the dishes and pottery can be adapted for embroidery designs.

patch-size pieces, especially luxury fabrics such as silks. Use these in miniature quilts, for covering buttons and folded flowers.

- Buy new to have the old: buy the man in your life a new tie, then talk him out of an old one.
- Recycle out-of-style but still good clothing into patch fabric.
- To solicit contributions, announce to friends and neighbors that you are collecting.

Using bias fabrics

When patches are laid onto a foundation, the grainline of the fabric becomes irrelevant. Because of this, bias fabrics, including men's ties, are easily used.

Also, when applied to a foundation, lightweight fabrics are much more stable.

Note: The "straight of grain" is the lengthwise grainline. It is necessary to use the "straight of grain" when cutting garment fabrics and patches for traditional quilting. The "cross grain" is the grainline from selvedge to selvedge.

Choosing Colors

At times, selecting a combination of coordinating colors is the most baffling aspect of crazy quilting. A basic understanding of color theory can be helpful.

Basic guidelines for using colors are taught to students of art and mastered by artists. First, let's study the visual appeal of some antique crazy quilts.

The Colors in Antique Crazy Quilts

The contrast is typically the most immediate recognizable characteristic of attractive antique quilts. The colors range from very light to very dark.

Characteristically, darks, lights and neutral shades are used nearly equally. This creates an overall balance. The appearance is easy to look at even though the maker used many colors. Also, there is usually a balance between warm and cool shades.

Bright golden yellow is used in some Victorian crazy quilts in occasional patches. It is also found in embroidery along the edges of a patch and was sometimes used as the sole color of embroidery thread. Bright golden yellow, used with other jewel-like and deep tones such as burgundy, dark green, violet, red and blue, adds a wonderful touch of contrast and brightness.

A lap quilt in roses, browns, cream, and antique gold will fit almost any home decor.

There is a balance between warm and cool colors (red and blue) in this antique wool quilt in which red predominates. Detail. The Brick Store Museum, Kennebunk, Maine.

As follows are the color schemes of two antique crazy quilts. The colors are separated into columns for easy comparison.

Quilt 1		
Darks	**Lights**	**Neutrals**
red/orange (rust)	antique gold	medium brown
black	gold	beige
orange	white	
blue	pink	
yellow-gold	pale blue	

Quilt 2		
Darks	**Lights**	**Neutrals**
black	soft yellow	medium brown
blue	yellow	light brown
purple	lt. orange	
red	pale blue	
olive		

Color pointers taken from antique quilts:

- Use vivid colors sparingly (magenta, royal blue, yellow, etc.). Separate with plenty of neutrals or with darker or lighter colors.
- To avoid a monotonous and dull appearance, separate similar shades (i.e. dusty rose and dusty blue) with lights or darks.
- Use a black patch to highlight nearby colors. Black patches in antique quilts were often embroidered with florals, scenes or even painted. The black background seems to highlight the incorporated colors.
- Shades of brown are useful in harmonizing surrounding colors. Browns tend to assume the depth of warm colors and the coolness of cool colors. This assumption thereby "extends" or "improves" a color scheme.

HERE IT IS IN A NUTSHELL

Dark and light,
Warm and cool,
Yellow's bright,
Brown's a tool.
Black is right,
Vivids duel!

This unusual circa mid-19th century quilt is made of many mauve, magenta, and purple fabrics. Some of the patches are set into a "sidewalk" pattern! Detail. The Brick Store Museum, Kennebunk, Maine.

Color Theory

Primary and Secondary Colors

The primary colors are red, blue and yellow, which are the basis for all other colors.

The secondary colors are obtained by mixing two primary colors, as shown in the diagram.

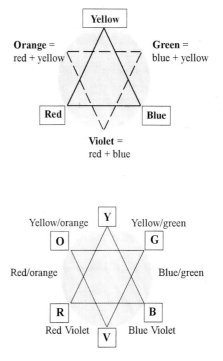

Tertiary Colors

As is evident in their names, the tertiary colors are obtained by mixing a secondary color with a primary: yellow/green, for instance, is made of yellow and green.

There are variations on each. For example, a yellow/green that tends toward yellow more than green is yellow/yellow/green.

Neutrals

Browns are created by various mixtures to result in yellow/brown, red/brown, taupe, violet/brown and others. These, in addition to gray, black and white, are called "neutral" colors.

Light and Dark Colors

Adding white (water if using dye) or black to a color stretches the range of possible colors. The color choices are nearly infinite.

Add white to create a lighter shade of any color. If dyes are used water creates a lighter shade of any color. The more white or water added to a color, the lighter the color.

Adding black to a color creates a darker color. The tiniest amount of black merely grays the color, while greater amounts deepen it more intensely.

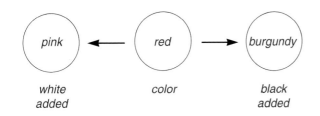

pink ← red → burgundy

white added   color   black added

Color Relationships

For the purpose of combining fabrics in a quilt, study the relationships between colors and their successful use.

Analogous colors share characteristics. Red, red-orange and orange are united by the varying degrees of red constituted by each color. Blue-green (peacock), green-blue (teal) and green are united by the common element of green. The analogous colors naturally blend. They easily complete a color scheme by the addition of lighter shades, darker shades and neutrals.

Complimentary colors have no shared characteristics. Red and green are commonly used complimentary

colors. The color green is obtained by mixing yellow and blue, neither of which appears in red–a primary or pure hue. Purple and yellow are complimentary (purple consists of red and blue and yellow is a pure hue), as are blue and orange (orange is yellow plus red and blue is a pure hue).

Complimentaries are easily found on a color wheel as direct opposites. There are also in-between complimentary hues, such as blue-violet and yellow-orange.

When placed near each other, complimentary colors tend to "clash" or reverberate. Use a complimentary to create vibrant areas in a quilt. In one antique crazy quilt I saw a fan pieced of royal blue and orange. Royal blue and orange is a striking combination! Tone down the colors to calm the vibrancy. For example, a soft combination is dusty rose used beside celery-green.

Cool colors include blues, purples and blue-greens. Cool colors tend to portray restful, calm, peaceful and relaxed feelings. Warm colors, indicative of action and passion, include reds, yellows, oranges and yellow-greens.

Neutral colors include shades of brown, gray, gray-browns (taupes), black and white. The browns are various mixtures of the pure hues mentioned above. Grays are mixtures of white and black.

When used between other colors in a quilt, browns and grays tend to create restful areas. Both prevent strong colors from overpowering. When placed between bright colors they create smooth transitions.

A balanced color scheme is the hallmark of this elegant mid- to late-19th century crazy quilt. Bright colors are softened by many neutrals. Detail. The Brick Store Museum, Kennebunk, Maine.

Observing Colors in Nature

We live in a colorful world! We are accustomed to an array of colors. How much do we actually think about them?

Many of us learned color "prejudices" at an early age. For instance, while in Kindergarten we were taught that tree trunks are brown. In reality, tree trunks are shades of gray, taupe and olive. Most unlike the blue crayon so diligently used, the colors of lake, ocean and sky are ever-changing.

Notice how nature interposes vast areas in shades such as green and blue. How much sky is there in comparison to everything else? How do these panoramas function as backdrops for the colorful accents of flowers and birds?

Looking into the distance, what happens to the colors of objects? Do they fade, pale or take on grayed shades?

Compare the effects on a particular scene on a gray day and a sunny day. Perhaps a scene through a window. What colors are shadows? Is there inspiration here to translate to a quilt, an embroidery for a patch or a color scheme?

My favorite place to observe colors is the flower garden. Each day there is something new to behold. From vivid spring crocus to heady panicled lilacs, followed by soft sprays of Baby's Breath blooming one day and fading the next, the garden is a summer-long orchestra of colors. When roses bloom, each petal is a wonder to observe. Late in summer, what a surprise when the yellow and black spider has spun its fabulous web overnight. And how a drop of dew glitters on the web. A sight to see! ... and to embroider, perhaps?

Compare the effect of a glossy-leafed plant to one with a soft, fuzzy leaf. Bring these textures to a quilt you are working on! How can you replicate them with fabric choices? Observe also the wildlife attracted to the garden. Birds and insects, butterflies, toads, each of these a study in colors and textures.

Interior decorating and clothing fads and fashions over the years have combined colors in different ways. These are also opportunities to observe and study colors. Everywhere you go, try to see how colors were used in the exteriors and interiors of buildings. Go to museums and look for how colors were once used in clothing and upholstery. Studying colors and textures will heighten your awareness and appreciation of them.

Garden spiders appear in late summer to spin their elegant webs.

Exercise: Have you ever said "I hate that color!" ? Or is there a color that is not "your" color and you won't use it - for anything? What color is it—chartreuse, fuschia, an off-shade of green, perhaps? Find a piece of fabric in that color. Choose surrounding patch colors that look pretty to you, using neutrals if none others will do. Add a bit of lace to soften, do a little embroidery on it—a small butterfly, perhaps, or some silk ribbon roses.

Do you find yourself beginning to like a color you once thought you didn't like or couldn't use? Continue this exercise with any other disliked colors. Believe it or not, your color horizons will expand. You will start to look at colors with an eye to "where and how can I use that shade?" instead of having a "yuck" reaction.

Foundation Piecing

One theory of crazy quilting is that these quilts are a result of other quilts being patched as they wore out. Another is that the scraps left over from sewing were used as they were, simply assembled into a quilt top. Both of these ideas have been disproved through studying the quilts and the advertising of suppliers of the time. I haven't come across any "over-patching" except that done in recent times as an attempt to preserve quilts. A set of partly finished blocks that were never assembled in my collection clearly shows that crazy patching was intentional. And, both patterns for patching blocks along with the embroidery stitches to put on them, and scrap bag packages of fabrics were sold specifically for crazy quilting.

The Whole-Quilt Style was used for this fancy Victorian crazy quilt, patched with many small patches. It measures 54 inches x 56-1/2 inches. Owned by Avalon Antiques; photographed at Arundel Antiques, Arundel, Maine. Photo by Paul Baresel.

It is likely that many influences inspired crazy quilting. In the Victorian times, people were exposed to ideas and inventions and new products on almost a daily basis. In England, the great Exhibition of 1851, housed in the temporary structure, The Crystal Palace, brought together examples of the arts and industries of many nations. This was Prince Albert's idea, a monumental event that drew phenomenal crowds, introducing people to many sights they had never seen before. Queen Victoria herself took a personal interest in things India, while trade with the Orient flourished and influenced western art and decorating trends.

Some believe that crazy patching may have been inspired by the crackled, aged glazes on antique pottery, cracked glass or ice. Whether it is related or not, the Japanese used a method of printing textiles using finely cut paper stencils held together by fine strands of silk which the printing ink ignored. The threads formed a grid of what could be seen as oddly-shaped patches, upon which is the design. There are many other possibilities that may have inspired the "crazed" look including paving stones, stone walls, and patterns in nature.

The Foundation

Except for the Confetti method, crazy quilting consists of applying patches of varying sizes and shapes onto a foundation, a piece of fabric the size of the quilt top or block. The type of foundation to use depends on the quilt or project being made. A foundation fabric should be chosen for the drape, warmth, weight, and firmness it will add to the finished quilt or project.

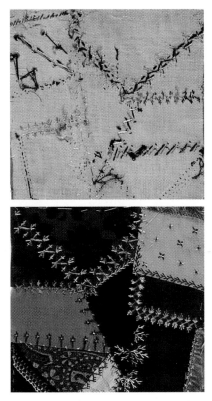

TOP PHOTO: The reverse side of a block from a crazy quilt that was never assembled clearly shows that foundation patching was intentional. The backs of the embroidery stitches, and some basting stitches indicate the Antique method of patching a crazy quilt; 9 inches square. Collection of the author.

BOTTOM PHOTO: The right side of the block.

Foundation Fabrics

Muslin

An excellent choice for beginners, 100-percent cotton muslin provides a firm base, and can be used for any type of crazy quilt, and any patching method. Keep in mind that it provides little drape if you are making a garment. Look for a quality muslin with an even grain. Cheaper muslins can come out unevenly in the wash (assuming the quilt will be washed) if the grain shifts or the fabric continually shrinks.

Batiste

A soft, finely woven, lightweight fabric, 100-percent cotton batiste is perfect for shawls, drapey quilts and clothing. To retain the drape, use soft and lightweight silks and cottons, and challis-type fabrics. Because of its softness, it is liable to bunching. This can be prevented by careful patching and pressing. The Antique or Landscape methods of patching are preferable for projects patched on batiste. Use an embroidery hoop for embroidery and embellishment.

Silk Organza

Crisp, loosely woven, and nearly weightless, silk organza is an ideal foundation for all-silk quilts. A substance from the silk worms creates a crispness that disappears when wet, and reappears as the fabric dries and is pressed. The fabric shrinks significantly in prewashing, so be sure to buy extra yardage. Lightweight silk patches placed onto it will retain their drape, making this an excellent base for silk crazy quilted clothing.

Since organza is loosely woven, use the Antique or Landscape method, squaring it up against a table edge or on a cutting mat to keep the grain even while patching. If you are making clothing, lay the pattern onto the piece periodically to check that it has not shifted out of place. After patching and basting, organza will hold its shape. Use an embroidery hoop for embroidery and sewn embellishments.

Flannel

Cotton flannel doubles as both a lightweight batting and foundation. A wool quilt pieced on flannel will be luxuriously warm, with a double-faced flannel adding slightly more loft than single-face. As with batiste, check often for bunching, because this fabric is soft, not crisp. Flannel is also an excellent choice for a jacket since it provides both drape and warmth. Any patching method can be used, taking care that the foundation stays smooth.

Fusible Interfacings

Fusing the patches to a 100-percent cotton fusible interfacing eliminates the need for basting. It is excellent for small projects such as handbags, book covers, and ornaments. I don't use it for quilts since the fusing unnaturally constricts fabrics, especially in a silk quilt since much of the beauty of silk is in its freedom of movement.

Preparing the Foundation

Prewash cottons in hot, soapy water. Wash silk organza by hand in warm water with mild soap. Rinse well, then line dry, and press. Trim off selvedges that bulge or prevent the foundation from lying flat. Cut the fabric to the size of the quilt top or block including a seam allowance of at least half an inch or more on each side. If the foundation must be pieced, instead of sewing a seam, overlap the raw edges and hand-stitch along the center of the overlap.

Quilt Sizes

Coverlets, throws, and lap robes are practical sizes for a crazy quilt. A coverlet can be the size of the top of the bed, or it can hang over the sides of the bed. Bed-size crazy quilts are easiest to make if the top is divided into blocks that are a convenient size to work on. Decide on the dimensions of the quilt, then choose a border width, and divide the remainder into blocks.

A throw can be about 50-60 inches square, and lap robes the size desired.

Any of these sizes can be used for wall hangings.

A foundation can be of any shape. This "butterfly" is thought to be an unassembled purse. Photographed at The Barn at Cape Neddick, Maine.

RIGHT: Detail of the cotton crazy quilt. Courtesy of The Kirk Collection, Omaha, NE. Photo by Nancy T. Kirk.

LEFT: This aged cotton crazy quilt consists of blocks separated by sashings. Note the border preceding the quilt's binding is not divided into blocks. Courtesy of The Kirk Collection, Omaha, NE. Photo by Nancy T. Kirk.

Quilt Styles

Antique crazy quilts were pieced as entire quilt tops, or were assembled of blocks. There was no standard size for blocks; they vary from one quilt to another from about 12 inches square to about 18 inches on average. To form the quilt top, the blocks were sewn together by machine or by hand. These seams were often finished with a simple row of Feather or Herringbone stitches on the face of the quilt.

Whole-Quilt Crazy Quilts

The Whole-quilt Method is useful for smaller quilts such as crib, lap robes, throws, and wall quilts. I like to use a square based on the width of the foundation fabric. In other words, a 44-inch wide fabric can be used to make a 44-inch square quilt.

This is about the largest size I like to work on. The Piano Shawl, Victorian, Ladies and Fans, and Butterstamp quilts are made this way (see Gallery).

Laying patches onto a foundation larger than this can get a little cumbersome, but working embroidery and embellishment on them can really prove daunting. Large quilts are much easier to work on if they are first divided into blocks.

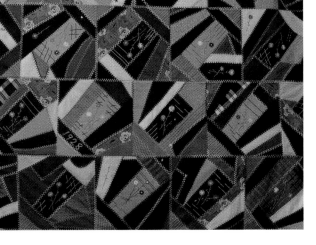

In this 1928 block-style wool quilt, the blocks are staggered. Collection of Rocky Mountain Quilts, York Village, Maine.

The Block Style of Crazy Quilting

For making large quilts, and for the Sew n' Flip method of patching, dividing the quilt top into blocks creates manageable portions. A large quilt can easily be made of blocks of any size. A 13-inch square of foundation will make a 12-inch block (1/2-inch seam allowances), a size that, for beginners, is easy to work on. I prefer blocks that are about 18-22 inches square.

The blocks do not have to be square, or all the same size, as long as they fit together in the end. A large central block can be surrounded by smaller ones. You can also make them as hexagons or diamonds if you like.

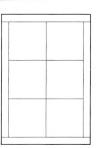

If you want the effect of a whole quilt, allow some patches to hang over the edges, then appliqué them later onto the adjoining blocks.

After the blocks are patched and embroidered, machine sew them with right sides together, then press the seams open. These seams can be embroidered with Feather or other stitching, taking care to keep the seam allowances open and flat.

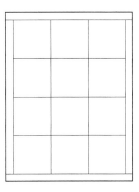

Blocks can also be assembled with sashing between them, as in the Cousins Quilt.

Crazy patches were machine stitched onto diamond-shaped blocks in this vintage crazy quilt. Collection of Rocky Mountain Quilts, York Village, Maine.

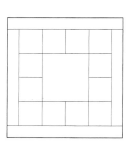

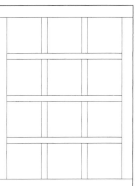

Patching the Crazy Quilt

Most antique crazy quilts were patched by hand, with the patches quilted to the foundation with embroidery stitches. This is the "Antique" Method given below. Patches can be arranged and rearranged, and an entire quilt top can be laid out before anything is fas-

This antique crazy quilt was made in long, narrow strips with velvet sashing between them. The sole embroidery is metallic chenille couched along patch edges. Note the softly rounded shapes of patches. Photographed at Gold Bug Antiques, Cape Neddick, Maine.

tened down. This method finishes to a softer appearance than machined seams, and also allows laces and trims to be added at any time before embroidering. Even though a seam may be already basted, it is easy to take out the basting, insert a trim, and then re-baste.

The "Sew n' Flip" machine method below is a common, modern method. However, embroidery has been 100 years in proving its proficiency in securing seams. In fact, on many deteriorated crazy quilts where some patches have long since disappeared, the embroidery stitches remain. There is no compelling reason to sew patches by machine unless you are making clothing that will be subjected to lots of wear and tear.

Each method has its own particular advantages. The Confetti Method can often be done the quickest, mostly because embroidery is not always needed. Choose a method that fits both the look you want to achieve and the purpose of the quilt.

Cutting Patches

Patches are not cut ahead of time. Cut each as it is needed according to the instructions for the method you are using.

What sizes to make the patches depends on personal prefer-ence, the project, and available fabric. My patch sizes are "quilt dependent," in other words larger for one quilt design, smaller for another, and mixed in yet others. If embroidery or embell-ishment will be added to the centers of the patches, be sure they are large enough for this. If you are a beginner, larger patches will be easier and reduce patching time. Mixing small and large patches creates variety.

Adding Laces and other Trimmings

Sew-on trims including laces, braids, ribbons, rick rack, cording, and so on should be added as the quilt is patched. Some of these must be inserted length-wise into a seam, while others have cut ends that must be concealed. Both types should be basted or sewn into patch seams.

Battenberg and crocheted motifs are excellent additions, and can be found in craft and sewing shops often in 4" to 12" rounds and heart shapes. The larger ones can be cut in half or in sections, and placed so that cut edges are secured in the patch seams.

Beautiful, heirloom-quality trims will add a touch of elegance to a crazy quilt! Cotton net lace, cotton and rayon Venice laces, cotton eyelet, and several narrow trims are shown here.

Bunching

Bunching is my term for patches and foundation that do not lie smoothly. Either the patch was not laid evenly, or the foundation shifted, causing fabrics to ripple, bulge, or pucker. Velvets, velveteens, and other napped fabrics are sometimes the culprits. It is also common when using a sewing machine where the feed dogs move the fabric along, but the presser foot does not, resulting in a slight unevenness between top and bottom fabrics. Allowing this to happen will tend to "shrink" the finished size of the piece being worked on, making it uneven, and causing a poor fit when blocks are assembled.

To prevent bunching, be sure the foundation remains absolutely smooth (lift your work and check it), pin carefully, hand baste (see "Basting," below), and press often. When using a sewing machine, hold the fabric firmly both in front of and behind the needle while sewing.

If bunching occurs regardless of your best efforts, then make your foundation an inch or so larger than needed. If it finishes too large, then trim it to size.

Pressing

Pressing is important for each of the methods below. It assists in getting patches to lie smoothly, eliminating puckering and bulging that could otherwise occur. Use a padded surface, or lay a terry cloth towel on the ironing board to prevent seam allowances making ridges on the surfaces of the patches. Press, do not iron. Pushing the iron about can dislodge patches, and get your iron full of pin scratches.

If a fabric gets a shine from pressing, then use a press cloth.

Patching Methods

Each of the following four methods comes out a little differently. A Potholder pattern follows, a small project with which you can try each of the methods.

Method 1. The Antique Method

This is the method that was most often used in antique crazy quilts. It allows for the greatest versatility in sizes and shapes of the patches. Curved shapes are easy to do, and make a softer looking quilt top than one with all angular pieces. It is sometimes easiest to begin at a corner, and work outwards from there. Patching can also be started in several different areas on the quilt, which come together as more patches are added. And, the entire quilt top can be patched before any stitching. This means you can work with the colors, re-arranging until the entire composition comes together.

❶ Begin by cutting and laying a patch wherever on the foundation you'd like to begin - at a corner, an edge, or in the center.

❷ Lay a second patch underlapping or overlapping it with the first by a 1/2 inch or a little more. Repeat with the third and fourth patches. After patching a section, continue with 3, or lay the patches on the entire quilt top or block, and then proceed with 3.

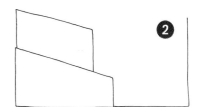

The Antique Method of patching.

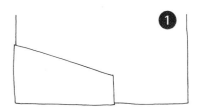

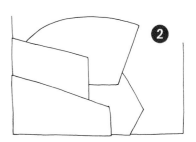

3 Go back to the first patch, and press under the overlapped edges about 1/4 inch, and pin. Continue for each patch, pressing and pinning. If there are any gaps, fit in another patch, replace a patch with a larger one, or add a piece of wide ribbon.

4 Pin on any trimmings desired, baste and embroider.

TIP: If patching becomes puzzling and you get confused over what to do next, here are some suggestions that may help.

• Take a break and come back later with a fresh mind.

• If you were painstakingly trying to fit small pieces together, set them aside and use one larger piece instead, or sew or baste several small ones together and then add them.

• Begin anew on a different area of the foundation, and work towards the original area.

Method 2. Landscape Patching

This is a methodical method that is a little easier than the "Antique" method, because there is no figuring out which edges will be turned under. Each patch is "finished" as it is added. All raw edges are either turned under or inserted under a previous patch. Patches having 90-degree or greater angles are preferred because their corners will finish more easily. Shapes with a rounded edge are also easy to use.

Patches may tend to "landscape," creating the effect of rolling hills or mountain ranges. Varying the sizes of patches, and making some long and narrow, and some more square-shaped can downplay this, or the effect can be used for a pictorial, scenic quilt.

The Landscape Method of patching.

Lay patches as if you were painting with fabric instead of paint. Arrange and re-arrange until the composition looks "right," then pin the fabrics in place. Trims are being added to this landscape piece.

This diagram shows a landscape patched block designed to achieve the effect of rolling hills. The dashed lines indicate patches that were pieced before being added to the block. Turn the page sideways, and then upside down to see the different effects that can be achieved by the orientation of the block.

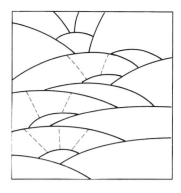

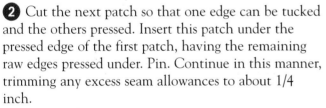

1 Beginning at one corner, cut a patch with a rounded edge, or a square with a corner removed. Press under its edges, except those that become the sides of the block.

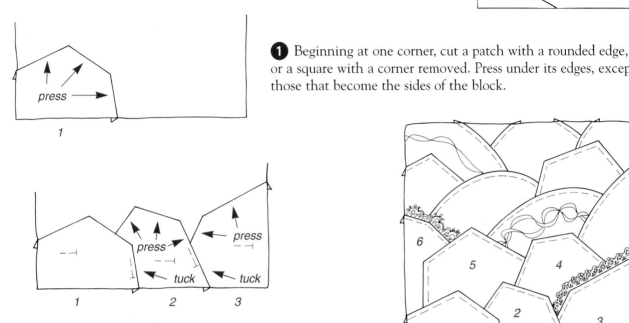

2 Cut the next patch so that one edge can be tucked and the others pressed. Insert this patch under the pressed edge of the first patch, having the remaining raw edges pressed under. Pin. Continue in this manner, trimming any excess seam allowances to about 1/4 inch.

3 Pin on any trimmings desired, baste and embroider.

Hand patching onto fusible interfacing

This is a difference in materials rather than method in which the step of basting is eliminated. Either patching method above can be used. Fusing the fabrics to interfacing creates a firm base for projects such as handbags and ornaments, in which small patches are used.

1 Substituting woven cotton fusible interfacing for the foundation fabric, have the fusible face upwards on your ironing board. Doing a small area at a time, fit a patch, then remove it from the foundation to press its edges under. Place it onto the fusible and pin. Repeat until the foundation is covered.

2 After all of the pieces are in place, fuse them, removing the pins as you press. Follow the directions with your fusible interfacing. The turned-under seam allowances that overlap onto adjoining patches will not be fused, but the patch itself will be held in place, and no further pinning or basting should be needed.

3 After fusing, trims can be inserted under the overlapped edges and basted. Finish with embroidery along patch edges.

TIP: Fusing can be used to create dimensional patches. Lay a patch-size piece of fusible face up on the ironing board. With a piece of lightweight fabric (such as silk), that is larger than the foundation, scrunch, fold, and tuck while pinning it onto the fusible. When finished, press to fasten it all down.

Basting

Basting can "make or break" a project. Done carefully, your quilt top or block will finish smoothly.

The patched block or quilt top should now be completely pinned, with trims added. Lightly press the pinned patches, making sure that everything lies smoothly. Double check that overlapping is sufficient, and no foundation shows through any gaps. Lift the entire piece to check that the foundation is smooth.

Basting is quickest and easiest if it is done on a smooth surface. To protect a table top, use a large rotary cutting mat. Do not use an unprotected dining table, it will get scratched! Lay the block or quilt top right side up on your working surface. Start in one area and work outwards.

Finger-pressing and removing pins, baste each turned-under edge. Stitches can be started and ended on the right side either with knots or one or two small stitches. Use extra pins and stitches to secure velveteen and any other napped patches.

Basting stitches can be of any size that results in a smoothly secured patch. Mine are about 1/2 inch in length.

If your block or quilt top tends to slide about on your working surface, weight it with books or other weights that won't harm the fabrics.

Patches and fans are basted and ready for embroidery in the Ladies and Fans quilt.

Techniques for Basting

1. Use a Sharp size 12, or other small-eyed needle.
2. Thread the needle with cotton sewing thread that is not doubled. Knot the end.
3. Take several stitches, then pull the thread through. Before each stitch, smooth the patch with your fingers, then hold fabrics down while pulling the thread through.

In stitching, the needle slides along the working surface.

Following these instructions, your basting should result in smooth, unpuckered patches and foundation, with no "shrinkage" of the piece. If a patch becomes distorted while basting, remove the stitches, press, pin, and baste again.

Method 3. Sew N' Flip

Machine Patching

Have your ironing board placed next to your sewing machine. You will want to work with blocks that are not too large or the work will quickly become difficult to handle. About a 10- to 12-inch square is a good size to begin with. Use a firm foundation such as muslin.

The Sew n' Flip Method.

1 Begin with a 5-sided patch at the center of the block. Pin. Lay a second patch onto the first with right sides together, and sew the seam leaving 1/4 inch unsewn at each end. Do not backstitch, since occasionally part of a seam may need to be opened up later on.

2 Add each patch in this manner, trimming out any excess from previous patches. Where edges cannot be sewn by machine, turn them under and press. These edges can later be slipstitched, or held in place with embroidery. Remember to add any trimmings that will be sewn into seam allowances.

3 It is easiest to have all patches straight-sided (no curved or shaped pieces), and cut into triangular or long, sloping rectangular shapes. As patches are added they often have a tendency to become larger or longer. Two or more patches can be pieced together before they are added.

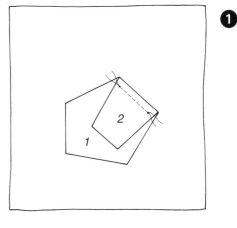

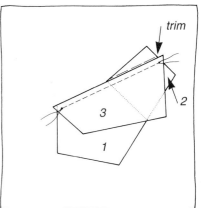

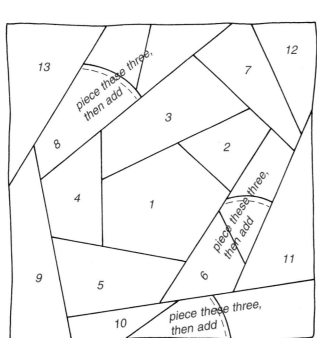

Method 4. "Confetti" Piecing

I enjoy this much more than the Sew n' Flip method. It is quicker, easy, and less puzzling. If you need to make something in a hurry, this is the method to use. It is done completely by machine, without a foundation, and results in all straight seams. Laces and trimmings are not sewn into the seams since they will create too much bulk. A great method for a kid's quilt, it makes a sturdy fabric that will hold up to washing and wear. Cotton fabrics are recommended. In order to understand how the method works, do a "test run" with scrap fabrics.

Use 1/4-inch seam allowances, pressing to one side.

The Confetti Method.

1 Sew together two large patches that are about 9 by 11 inches or so. Press. Add a patch to each end as shown in the following diagram, sew, and press.

2 Cut the piece in half along a straight line. To obtain a straight line, fold the piece and press a crease, or use a pencil and a ruler.

3 Turn the two pieces, and re-join by sewing, having right sides together. Press.

4 Cut again, and rejoin. When rejoining pieces, it is not necessary to rejoin at an edge. With right sides together, add anywhere onto the piece, then trim off the excess. Rejoin the trimmed-off piece to another area.

To have more than four colors, make two pieces as in 1, using different colors for each. Sew them together, then cut and rejoin. Do this several more times to scramble the two parts.

Finish to have as near a square as possible.

To form a square block, cut a piece of foundation or paper the size of the block, including seam allowances. Align the foundation or paper on top of the sewn piece so it most nearly covers it. Trim off any edges that protrude. Sew the trimmed pieces back on, and continue until the sewn piece is the same size as the block.

Make the required number of blocks for your quilt.

Embroidery along patch seams is optional especially if the patches are very small. A few plain feather stitches can be worked along some of the major seams if desired, although if printed fabrics were used, the quilt may be fancy enough. If the piece will be embroidered by hand or by machine, first baste a piece of foundation to the back of it to cover the seams.

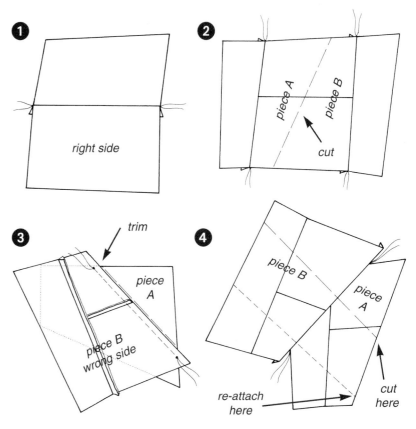

Making a Pattern

For all patching methods except Confetti, a pattern can easily be made for the patches on a block. You can use one pattern for all of the blocks in a quilt, making each look different with embroidery and embellishment, and turning them to face in different directions when assembling the quilt top. Otherwise, a pattern can be drawn for each block, each with its own patch arrangement.

Patterns can be made, or blocks can be patched simply as in this antique wool quilt. These blocks are about 11-1/2 inches square. Detail. Owned by Avalon Antiques, photographed at Arundel Antiques, Arundel, Maine. Photo by Paul Baresel.

To make a pattern:

1 You will need a piece of paper the size of the finished block (without seam allowances). You may need to tape sheets of paper together first.

2 Using the Victorian Stitches plates in the following chapter for block ideas, sketch patch outlines onto the paper. Use a ruler for the straight lines, and freehand the curves. Erase and re-work lines until you have a balanced arrangement.

3 Number each patch. On a separate sheet of paper, sketch a small diagram showing the approximate shapes of the patches, and enter the numbers given each. Set aside the diagram.

4 Cut out the paper patches. Place them onto the patch fabrics with right sides up. Adding a seam allowance of at least 1/4 inch around each, cut out the patches.

5 Cut out the foundation fabric adding a seam allowance of 1/2 inch all around. Following the diagram, place each patch in its numbered place on the foundation.

Continue according to the patching method of your choice.

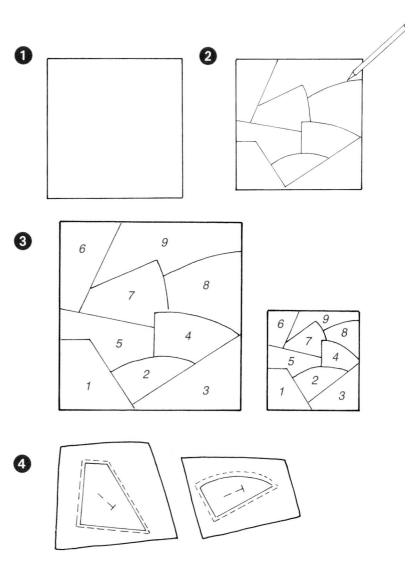

Patched and ready for embroidery and embellishment, the Ladies and Fans quilt-in-progress is clothespinned to hangers for viewing.

Viewing Your Work

After the patches are basted onto the foundation of a quilt top or block, I like to hang up the piece, to be able to view it from a distance. An easy way to do that is to clip it to coat hangers using smooth spring-type clothespins. Use as many hangers as needed, and bend the tops so they fit over a door or curtain rod. This is also a good way to store the piece when you are not working on it. Be sure to keep your work out of direct sunshine and away from heat sources.

Potholders Pattern

This pattern is for making four potholders, a small format for trying each of the above patching methods. After making one block of each, it will be easier to decide which to use for quilts and other projects.

Finished size of each: 8-1/2-inches square

Materials:

four 9-inch squares of muslin for foundation
eight or more cotton patch fabrics
cotton laces as desired for methods 1, 2, and 3
four 9-inch squares of 100-percent cotton batting
four 9-inch squares of cotton or linen backing fabric
size 8 pearl cotton, 8 or more colors
five yards of 1/2-inch wide double fold bias tape, matching
  thread

Use a 1/4-inch seam allowance throughout.
Instructions:
1 If desired, round the corners of each muslin, and also those of the batting and backing pieces. Apply patches to each using the Antique method for one, Landscape for another, and Sew n' Flip for the third. Add cotton laces as desired. Construct a fourth using the Confetti method, basting the foundation on afterwards.
2 Embroider, following instructions for Victorian Stitches following. The Confetti potholder may be left plain, or several rows of feather-stitching can be worked along major seams.
3 Assemble the layers with wrong sides together; quilted top, then batting, followed by backing, and pin. Sew a loop for each potholder made of the bias tape, and baste to one corner of each, or add a bone ring afterwards.
4 Open out the bias tape and sew it with right sides together about 1/4 inch from the edge of the potholder. Ease the bias at the corners so it will turn smoothly. Overlap and fold the raw end under. Fold the bias to the back, press, and slipstitch.

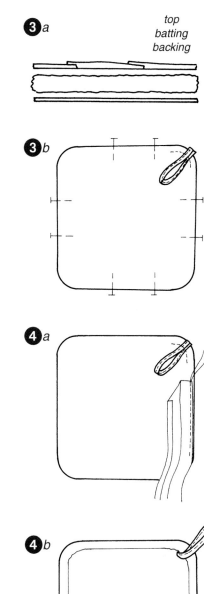

Victorian Stitches

Both practical and aesthetic, the rows of embroidery stitches along the patch seams of antique crazy quilts fasten the patches to each other, and at the same time quilt them to the foundation fabric. Although many Victorian crazy quilts featured a single row of feather or herringbone stitches along each seam, the more beautiful ones have a wide variety of stitches, and sometimes multiple rows along each seam. The jewel-like patterning of some of these fancier quilts makes them almost seem to sparkle.

According to Betsey Telford of Rocky Mountain Quilts in York, Maine, the mark of excellence in Victorian crazy quilting was for the needleworker to make at least one hundred different embroidery stitches on a quilt. I think where they ran out of stitches, they made them up!

This detail of a circa 1880's crazy quilt shows a range of embroidery stitches. The Brick Store Museum, Kennebunk, Maine.

Threads for Crazy Quilting

When I first began crazy quilting more than 12 years ago, there were only a few variety threads available, and they were hard to find. Now, there are so many it can be difficult to choose, a clear indication of the unrivaled growth of interest and creativity in the needlearts!

Collect a variety of the wonderful thread types available, and try them. You're sure to find some that will become your favorites.

Threads follow the same fiber descriptions as those given for fabric types in chapter two. As with fabrics, the natural fibers silk, cotton, wool, and the earliest synthetic, rayon, can be found in various types and finishes. Synthetic and variety threads are also available including those with metallic shine, and some that are "borrowed" from the knitting department such as chenille and kid mohair.

Silk, rayon, and metallic threads are spun of many shorter fibers, or made of long, singular filaments. Cotton and wool threads are always spun, since their fibers by nature are short. Spun fibers are usually more matte in finish, while filaments display more sheen.

TIP: A Ply is a ply, and a strand is a strand. These two terms are often confused with each other. A ply is a single fiber or thread made of a filament such as silk or rayon, or spun of shorter fibers such as cotton or wool. As an example, sewing thread is one strand, however, when you untwist the end, you can see that the thread divides into separate plies. Plies are not normally meant to be separated.

A strand is one thread of several that are placed together to form a multi-strand skein such as six-strand embroidery floss. Each strand may consist of several plies.

Both twist and number of plies give a thread its strength.

Working with Silk Threads

Twisted types such as Soie Perlee can snag, pulling one ply loose, and causing the thread to appear to disintegrate right before your eyes. If this should happen, hold the thread vertically and drop the needle to the base, where it comes through the fabric. Run your fingers upwards along the thread several times, smoothing it until the plies become even. Bring the needle back up and continue stitching.

Stripping is a way of preparing silk floss for embroidery when more than one strand is used in the needle. Cut a working length of the floss, and individually pull out as many strands as will be used, then lay them smoothly back together again. This allows the full sheen of the thread to show, and helps embroidery stitches such as Satin Stitch lie smoothly. Cotton and rayon flosses also benefit from stripping.

Working with Rayon Threads

Twisted rayon threads such as Pearl Crown benefit from giving the thread a quick snap. First, cut a working length of thread, then hold both ends of it and give a sharp tug, just enough to relax the thread. This helps prevent tangling.

Rayon flosses should be stripped the same as silks as explained above. Some rayon threads, especially skeined flosses appear "kinky" as they are removed from a skein. To remove the kinks, run the thread over a damp paper towel and allow it to dry before using.

Tangling

Tangling can occur with any threads used in hand stitching. Hold up your work and allow the thread to dangle and untwist occasionally. Also, as you embroider, place your left thumb (if you are right-handed) on the thread about 1 inch from where it comes through the fabric. Then, as the stitch is made, release the thread at the last instant.

The "Stab" Method

If threads tend to wear quickly as they are pulled through fabrics, do not "sew" them. Make the stitch in parts, first bringing the needle down through the fabric and pulling the thread through. Then bring the needle up and pull through.

Preparation of Hands

Anyone who enjoys both gardening and embroidery knows that you can't just pick up your embroidery upon coming in from the garden. Threads, especially silks and rayons will snag on rough fingers and fingernails.

Thickly apply a non-greasy hand lotion, rub it in thoroughly, then buff your hands on a clean towel until they feel smooth and dry. Keep an emery board with your sewing things to smooth rough spots on your fingers and nails that appear while stitching.

Thread types

Twisted Threads for Patch Seam Embroidery.

There are three thread types I use almost exclusively for patch seam embroidery. These are Size 8 Pearl Cotton, Soie Perlee, and Pearl Crown Rayon. These can be mixed and matched on one quilt, or used cotton on cotton, silk on silk, and rayon thread on rayon patch fabrics.

Pearl cotton is an all-cotton thread available in a wide color range in skeins or larger spools. Size 8 is ideal for crazy patch embroidery. Pearl cottons are available in other weights including the finer Size 12, and the heavier Size 5. There are several different manufacturers of this thread.

My favorite silk thread for crazy patch embroidery is Soie Perlee, ideal for embroidery on fancy or silk crazy quilts. Slightly finer than the Size 8 Pearl Cotton, it comes on 11-yard spools. It is a modern-day counterpart to the silk buttonhole twist once available from Belding Corticelli. The buttonhole twist seems to have gone out of style, with buttonholes seldom made by hand anymore. Twisted silks are also available

Twisted threads impart an unrivaled texture and definition to stitches worked along patch seams. Included here are Kreinik Soie Perlee and Silk Serica®, DMC® size 8 pearl cotton, Pearl Crown Rayon, Needle Necessities' Pearl 8 Overdyed.

in other weights, such as the finer Soie Gobelin, ideal for miniature work and fine outline embroidery, and the heavier Silk Serica®, similar to Size 5 Pearl Cotton.

Pearl Crown Rayon is a twisted 100-percent rayon thread available on 100-yard spools, and similar in thickness to the Size 8 Pearl Cotton. I like this thread for its high sheen, and find it excellent for most quilts. Fewer colors are available, but it can be used in combination with other thread types. It has a high sheen and shows up brilliantly.

Threads for Other Uses

Flower thread is a matte-finish twisted cotton similar in weight to Size 12 Pearl Cotton. Use it for fine outline embroidery, miniature crazy quilts, monograms, cross stitch embroidery, and sampler work. Flower thread and Size 12 Pearl Cotton were used to embroider the Kate Greenaway figures on the Cousins quilt.

Flosses are multi-stranded skeined threads that can be separated for use, and are available in cotton, silk, rayon, wool, or metallic fibers. In crazy quilting, flosses are excellent for Satin Stitch embroideries on patch centers, and useful as the filler thread for couching. Flosses are not the best threads for patch edge embroidery, since the stitches will not be well defined, lacking the texture of twisted threads.

A collection of threads for hand embroidery including flosses: Kreinik's Soie D'Alger, The Caron Collection Waterlilies®, DMC® Rayon Floss.
Flower threads: The Caron Collection's Wildflowers®, DMC® Flower Thread , Wool threads: Impressions®(wool/silk), Needle Necessities' Overdyed French Wool; DMC® Medici wool, Paternayan® Persian wool.

Wool threads can be used for wool embroidery, punchneedle, needlepoint, and embroidery along patch seams in wool crazy quilts. Paternayan® Persian wool, spun for crewel embroidery and needlepoint, is an excellent thread for these purposes. DMC® Broder Medici, and Needle Necessities' Overdyed French Wool are finer threads in multi-stranded skeins ideal for outline, satin stitch, or single-strand fine embroidery.

Some knitting wools can be used for embroidery. Test them by working some embroidery stitches to be sure they are strong enough. Those that are loosely spun, although fine for knitting, will pull apart if used for embroidery. Any knitting wool can be couched.

Metallic threads often consist of a tinsel-like strand that is spun, plied, or wound around a core of nylon or other fiber. There are many different makes and types, from one-ply filaments to twisted threads and flosses, cordings, and ribbons in different weights and thicknesses. "Blending filaments"

are extremely fine and are meant to be knotted into the needle alongside a second thread of another type.

Rarely do metallics embroider easily. Use short lengths for those that can be pulled through fabric. Metallic threads can be couched to make wonderful spiderwebs!

Linen threads with their unique luster used mainly for hardanger and lacemaking, can also be used creatively in embroidery. Green Mountain Hand-dyed Linens offers linen threads that are

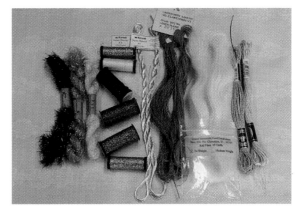

Some variety threads can be sewn through fabric, others can be couched. From left to right: Needle Necessities' Charleston, Kreinik metallic ribbons and Japan Gold, Green Mountain's hand-dyed linen thread and Kid Mohair, and DMC® metallic flosses.

hand dyed in natural dyes in a range of exquisite colors.

Yarns made of exotic fibers from angora (bunny), alpaca, mohair (goat), and other animals can often be found in knitting shops. Use them in creative embroideries, for portraying animals, and for couching along patch seams. As with any knitting yarns, be sure they are strong enough for embroidery.

Chenille is a yarn with a pile spun into its core threads. Very popular Victorian embroidery materials, chenilles were couched as filler in embroideries, and along seams of crazy patches. Victorian instructions say to test them for strength before using. Now, as then, run them through your fingers to be sure they hold together well.

Learning the stitches

Most embroidery stitches are easy to learn, although some may appear more complicated than they actually are. Beginners can learn the stitches in the following order from simple to more complicated: Running and Straight, Blanket, Fly, Chain, Lazy Daisy, Outline, Feather, Herringbone, Fishbone, French Knot, Bullion.

On scrap fabric, try making each stitch in very small to very large sizes, then it will be easier to settle on an appropriate size for your own preference. Practice each stitch many times until you feel comfortable and at ease with it.

Scatter your stitching over a quilt top or block, rather than beginning in one area and moving on from there. That way, one area will not stand out if your stitching changes. The same technique can be used to evenly distribute a thread color over a quilt top.

Beginners often find it difficult to make stitches evenly in rows. This is easier if you establish a rhythm as you work. It is often, however, the unevenly-

RIGHT: This Oriental silk embroidery is a gorgeous example of satin stitch embroidery. Collection of Paul Baresel.

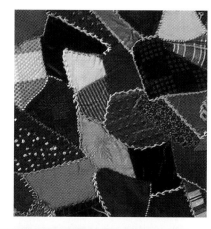

LEFT: If you learn only one stitch, such as the plain Feather Stitch, that is all you really need to complete a quilt top. After achieving proficiency with one stitch, try learning another. Antique block, 9 inches square; collection of the author.

LEFT: The creative uses of the Outline stitch on this 1898 quilt make it stand out. The flowers on the patches and the border design are all worked in this stitch. Collection of the author.

RIGHT: One way to learn the stitches is to work them on an even-weave fabric, using the weave to help make even stitches. This sampler of crazy-quilting stitches was done in size 8 pearl cotton, with the monogram worked in size 12, and embellished with Whimsey seed beads and glass heart beads from Wichelt Imports, Inc. The background fabric is the color, "Spun Silver," a 28-count 100-percent linen also from Wichelt Imports, Inc.

made stitches that are most interesting to look at. Unevenness also becomes less visible as more stitching is added to the quilt.

Thread lengths to use depends on how well a thread holds up to being pulled through the fabric. Use short lengths of about 18 inches for most metallics, silks, and some rayons. Most cottons can be used in one-yard lengths.

If a thread frays at the eye of the needle, pull it a little through the needle and trim off the frayed end. Be sure the needle's eye is smooth. If not, discard the needle.

Ripping out is an essential part of doing needlework of almost any type. If you don't like the stitches you've made, it's better to re-do them or start over with a different stitch or thread. If you leave them in, they will be the focal point of the quilt every time you look at it, although others will be less likely to notice.

About Machine Embroidery

Although antique crazy quilts were embroidered by hand, machine embroidery can be done on modern crazy quilts. Almost any type of sewing machine can be used. The many different techniques include using a heavier thread or silk ribbon in the bobbin (sewn with the piece upside down), free-form darning with the feed dogs lowered, appliqué, couching, cording, built-in embroidery stitch cams, computerized and programmable embroidery stitches, and so on. If you'd like

to try this, your machine's manual will specify what your machine can do.

Machine stitching has a much different character to that of handwork. Try working small samples of each to compare the difference. The machine pulls the layers of fabric tightly together, and places a great many stitches where hand embroidery uses many fewer. Closely placed zig zagging, a common form of machine embroidery, results in a hard, flat surface, compared to the soft and flexible dimensionality of hand stitches. You can choose a method based on either your preference or the use of the finished project.

Catherine Carpenter of Massachusetts designed and stitched a true labor of love in a needlework created for her granddaughter, Leah C. Carpenter. This waterfall detail demonstrates proficient use of basic embroidery stitches. Photo by Richard Carpenter.

The benefits of hand embroidery.

Some years ago, I spent hours running the sewing machine at high speed to quilt a kimono jacket by zig zagging narrow rayon ribbons onto it. Since then, I've put the machine aside and have embroidered over a dozen quilts, a jacket, and many small projects by hand. And I'm fully convinced that hand embroidery has advantages that machine work cannot touch. These include the pleasures and comforts of stitching away while sitting in the sun in a backyard Adirondack chair, a Victorian rocker on the front porch, in front of the TV in the parlor, my studio on a Sunday morning listening to jazz, and even on camping trips seated on the ground. This is embroidery as it was many years ago, in the company of family and friends.

Note the unusual stitches on this antique crazy quilt block! Collection of Rocky Mountain Quilts, York Village, Maine.

Embroidery Stitch Instructions

Blanket Stitch and Related Stitches

BLANKET STITCH—Come up through the fabric at A, and stitch from B to C. The thread is kept under the needle. Working towards the right, stitch from D to E for the following stitch. Repeat. End a row with a short tacking stitch.

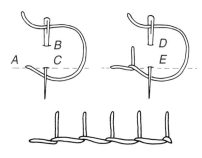

BUTTONHOLE STITCH—Work the same as for the Blanket Stitch, making the stitches very close together.

BLANKET FAN—This is easiest to work upside-down. Use the same hole in the fabric for the top of each stitch, making as many stitches as desired. Finish the fan with a Straight stitch.

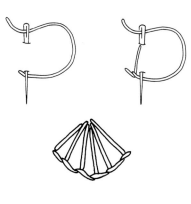

Blanket stitching was used to secure heart-shaped appliqués, in addition to patch-seam embroidery.

CLOSED OR CROSSED BUTTONHOLE —Slant the upper parts of the stitches together in pairs, meeting at the top for the Closed, and overlapping for the Crossed Buttonhole.

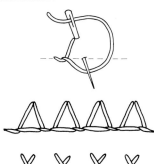

DETACHED BUTTONHOLE—Make a Straight Stitch, then work Buttonhole Stitch onto it without piercing the fabric. The Buttonhole Stitch can be worked onto any existing stitch, such as Straight stitch with one making a delicate leaf, and several worked in a circular fashion making a rose.

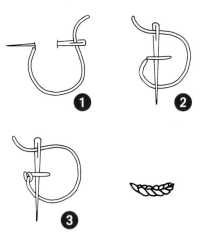

EYELET—Draw a small circle inside a larger one on the fabric. Work the Buttonhole stitch around.

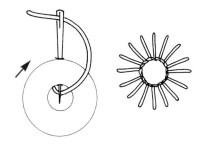

KNOTTED BUTTONHOLE—Wrap the thread once around the needle in the opposite direction of a French Knot, pull snug, and finish the stitch.

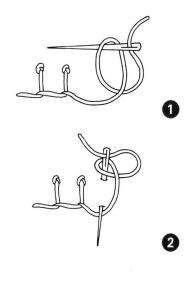

The Bullion stitch lends itself well to wool embroidery, as here on the Horses and Roses quilt.

BULLION KNOT–It may take a few tries to learn these, but once you do, they are both fun and easy to make. Come through the fabric at A. Insert the needle from B to A, do not pull through. Wrap the end of the needle evenly enough times to cover the distance between A and B. Hold onto the wraps while pulling the needle through, and continue to hold them until the thread is completely pulled through. Bring the needle down at B. The wraps may be adjusted by tugging on the thread slightly, or by stroking the stitch with the needle.

BULLION ROSE–Begin with three short Bullions placed in a triangle. Surround them with longer Bullions in a circular fashion.

LOOPED BULLION–Make the wrapped part of the stitch at least twice as long as the distance between A and B.

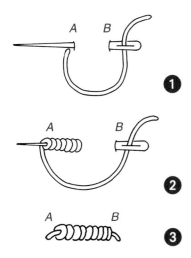

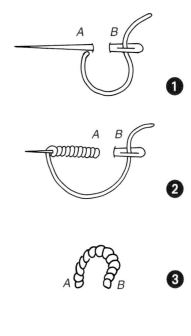

CHAIN STITCH–Come through the fabric at A, and stitch from B to C. Repeat as shown, working towards the left. End with a short tacking stitch.

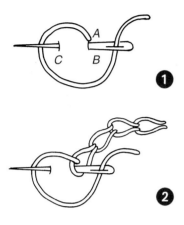

CHAIN STITCH ROSE–Beginning at the center, work the Chain Stitch in a circular fashion until the rose is the size desired.

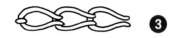

CABLE CHAIN–Make one Chain Stitch, wrap the thread once around the needle, pull snug, and make the following Chain Stitch not into the first stitch, but just past it. If you are accustomed to making the French Knot, wrap this stitch in the opposite direction.

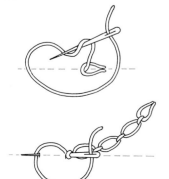

The Chain Stitch and variations of it form an excellent base for additional stitches.

MAGIC CHAIN–Thread the needle with two different types or colors of thread. Working the Chain Stitch, separate the two threads and use one of them to make the first stitch, then the other for the following stitch. Repeat.

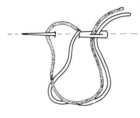

OPEN CHAIN–Come up at A, then stitch from B to C. To begin the following stitch, insert the needle at D, and repeat. End with two tacking stitches to hold the loop open.

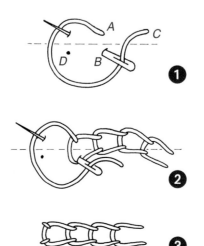

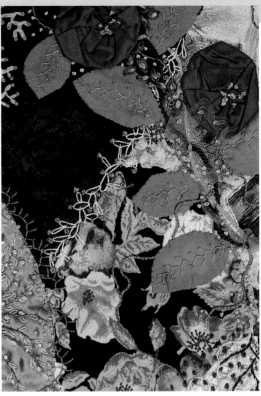

TWISTED CHAIN STITCH–Come up on the line at A. Stitch from B to C having the thread go over, then under the needle. Repeat.

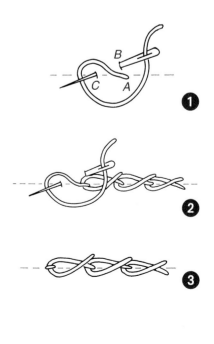

CORAL
STITCH–Make
a short slanting
stitch, having
the thread go
over, then
under the nee-
dle. Keep the
thread snug
while pulling
through.
Repeat, work-
ing towards the left.
CORAL KNOT–Make a short,
vertical stitch, wrap the thread
over, then under the needle.
Pull snug, and pull through.
Finish with a short tacking
stitch. These can be made in a
row, or scattered.

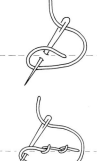

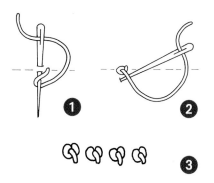

CORAL KNOTTED
HERRINGBONE–First make a row
of Herringbone Stitch. Fasten
on a second thread and work
Coral Stitch over the crossed
parts of the Herringbone without piercing the fabric.

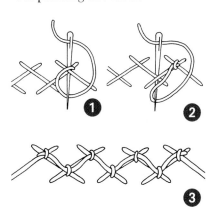

*The Zigzag Coral stitch in the
Ladies and Fans quilt.*

KNOTTED CABLE CHAIN
STITCH–this is a combination of
Coral, lacing, and Chain stitch.
1. Come up at A, and stitch
from B to C to make a Coral
Knot. 2. Slide the needle under
the thread between A and B
without piercing the fabric, and
pull through. 3. Insert the needle at D, come up at E having
the thread go under the needle.
Repeat from 1.

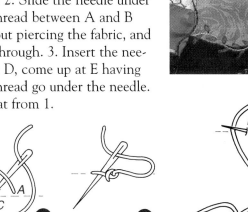

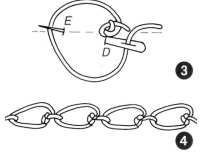

LONG-ARMED SINGLE CORAL
STITCH–Make these in rows,
clusters, or individually. 1.
Come up on the line at A.
Insert the needle from B to C,
do not pull through. Wrap the
thread over, then under the
needle as shown. Pull snug,
then bring the needle through.
2. Go down at D, just beneath
the stitch.

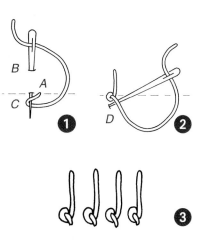

ZIG ZAG CORAL STITCH–1.
Make a Coral Stitch at the top
of the row. 2. Wrap the thread
over the needle, then make a
second Coral Stitch wrapping
the thread in the opposite
direction as shown. Repeat
from 1.

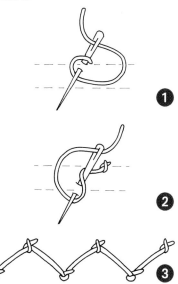

COUCHING. Fasten on the thread to be couched, or secure its ends under patch seams. With a second thread, stitch over the couched thread and through the fabric. Use short Straight stitches, or any embroidery stitch that will secure the couched fibers.

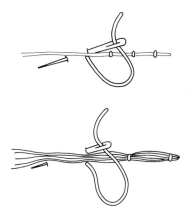

Couching with French Knots and buttons holds ribbons in place on the Victorian quilt.

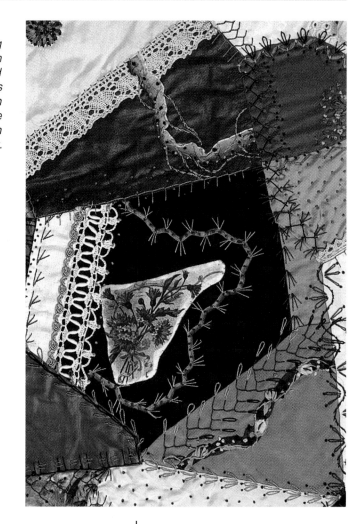

FILLER COUCHING–Long stitches used to fill in an area can be couched at intersections or at intervals to hold them in place.

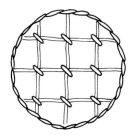

SHEAF STITCH–Make three vertical Straight Stitches, then make a short tacking stitch in the middle.

THORN STITCH–1. Make a long stitch of a heavy thread, shaping it into a curve. 2. With a lighter thread, come up at A, and stitch from B to C, then go down at D. Repeat, spacing the stitches as evenly as possible.

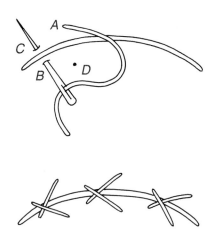

CRETAN STITCH. Working vertically, come up at A. 1. Stitch from B to C with the thread under the needle. 2. Stitch from D to E. Repeat 1 and 2, working first to one side, then the other of an imaginary line, always having the needle pointed towards the center of the stitching. This stitch can be worked closely or spread apart.

The Cretan stitch is one of several that make an ideal base row along patch and border seams.

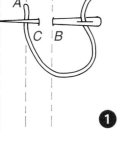

❶

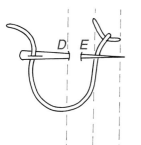

❷

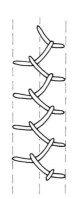

❸

CLOSED CRETAN—Begin by drawing a leaf shape onto the fabric, then follow instructions for the Cretan Stitch, beginning narrow and widening at the center.

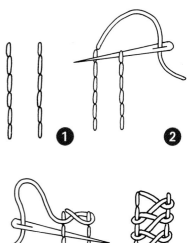

❶

❷

❸

RAISED CRETAN—work two rows of backstitch evenly. Without piecing the fabric work the Cretan Stitch between them. The backstitches can be arranged to form leaf shapes.

❶   ❷

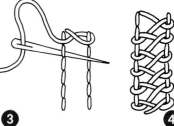

❸   ❹

CROSS STITCH. Come up at A, then down at B. Then come up at C and go down at D to make a Single Cross Stitch. To form a row of Cross Stitch, work the A to B part of the stitch across the row, turn, and work back along the row with the C to D part of the stitch.

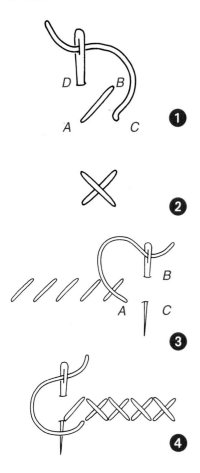

MOSS STITCH–This stitch was invented by Marion Nichols, the author of *Encyclopedia of Embroidery Stitches* (see Bibliography). 1. Make one Cross Stitch as above, bringing the needle up at A, above the stitch. 2. Form a loop, then place the needle over the loop and under the cross stitch without piercing the fabric. Pull

through and go down at B below the stitch.

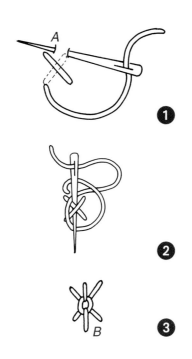

VICTORIAN FRINGE STITCH–Double the thread in the needle. Fasten on to the back of the fabric and bring the needle up between A and B. 1. Hold the thread with your thumb as shown, and stitch from A to B. 2. Then stitch from C to D, and bring the needle down at A. Begin the following stitch between B and E, and use the same holes as B and D. Keep the stitches consistent in size. The loops can be left as they are, or trimmed.

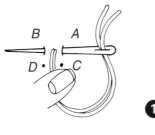

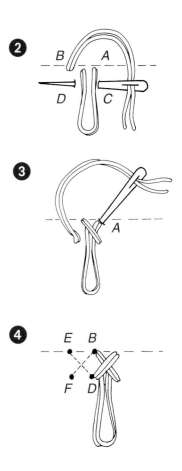

STAR STITCH–Make one Cross Stitch on top of another as shown. A small tacking stitch can be added at the center. Make the "arms" of equal or unequal length.

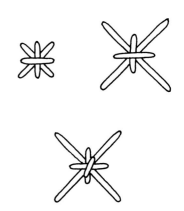

FEATHER STITCH. Working vertically along an imaginary line, come up at A. 1. Make a short, slanting stitch from B to C having the thread under the needle. 2. Make the following stitch from D to E, and repeat 1 and 2. End with a short tacking stitch.

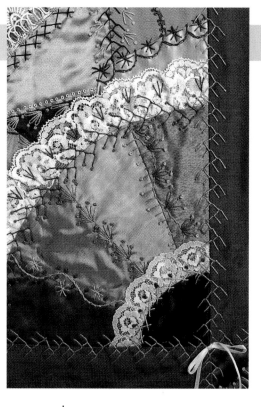

Feather Stitch is an excellent stitch for patch and border seams.

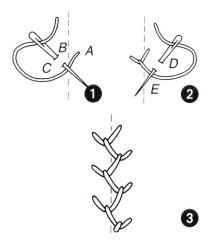

CHAINED FEATHER STITCH—This stitch consists of Long-stemmed Lazy Daisy Stitches in a Feather Stitch formation. Make a Lazy Daisy Stitch, then bring the needle down at the end of the stem, and up at the top of the next Lazy Daisy. Repeat.

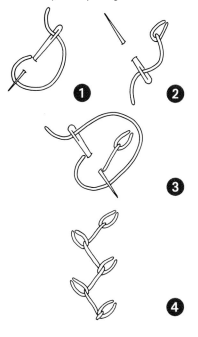

DOUBLE FEATHER STITCH—Begin the same as for the Feather Stitch, then make an extra "arm" on each side of the stitch. A triple feather can be made by adding yet another "arm" to each side. The arms are worked the same as Blanket Stitch.

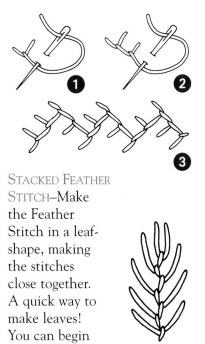

STACKED FEATHER STITCH—Make the Feather Stitch in a leaf-shape, making the stitches close together. A quick way to make leaves! You can begin by drawing a leaf shape onto the fabric, or make them freehand.

STRAIGHT-SIDED FEATHER STITCH—Make this stitch the same as the Feather Stitch, but with vertical "arms."

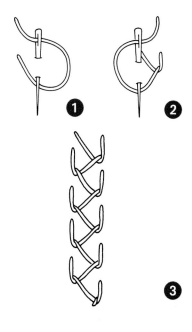

FERN STITCH. There are two ways to make this stitch. It is more quickly formed by beginning with a vertical Straight Stitch followed by a series of Fly stitches.

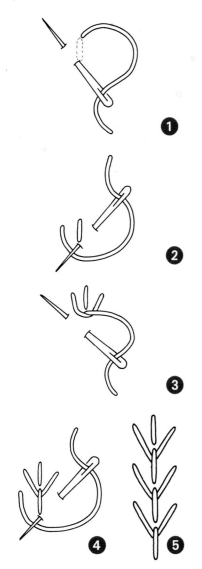

The Fern Stitch is used around an appliqué on the Butterstamp Quilt.

STRAIGHT STITCH FERN–Arrange triads of Straight Stitches one above another.

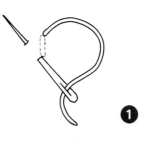

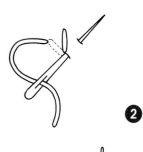

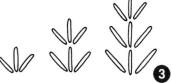

FISHBONE STITCH. First, make a vertical Straight Stitch. Then come up at A, and stitch from B to C. The following stitch is made in the same way in the opposite direction. The stitches will overlap slightly along an imaginary center line.

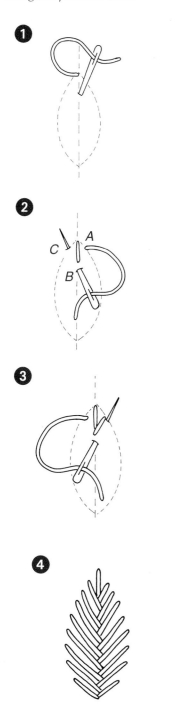

The Closed Fishbone Stitch is used for placing leaf shapes along patch seams, and with roses.

OPEN FISHBONE–This is easiest done by following a drawn line on the fabric. Bring the needle up at A, just to the left of the line. 1. Stitch from B to C. 2. Stitch from D to E having the thread over the needle. 3. Repeat from 1, working downwards.

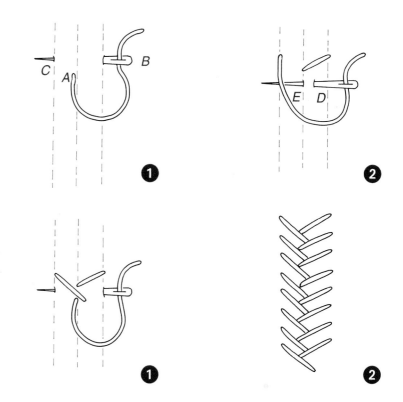

FLY STITCH. Come up at A, and stitch from B to C. Finish with a short tacking stitch. The Fly Stitch can be varied by making the tacking stitch differently–use a French Knot, a small Lazy Daisy, or continue the tacking stitch into Outline stitch.

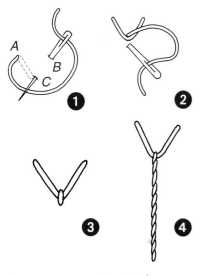

LONG-STEMMED FLY–Make a longer tacking stitch.

Fly Stitch is one of few stitch types used on this 1898 crazy quilt. These are scattered on a patch. Detail. Collection of the author.

CROWN STITCH–Make a wide and shallow Long-stemmed Fly, then add two Straight Stitches.

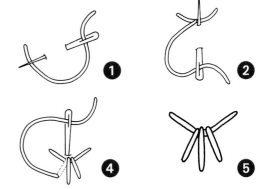

TETE DE BOEUF–This is actually Fly Stitch that is tacked with a Lazy Daisy stitch. The name means "head of the bull." It is sometimes called "Wheat-ear" Stitch.

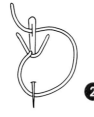

STACKED FLY STITCH–Make a series of Fly stitches vertically.

FRENCH KNOT. 1. Come up at A. Wrap the thread around the needle once, pull snug. 2. Bring the needle through the fabric at B. Follow the direction of the thread as shown. If wrapped in the wrong direction, the stitch can slip through and disappear. Wrapping the thread two, three or more times around the needle will make a larger stitch.

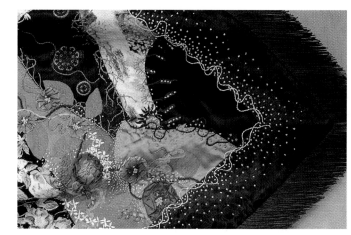

A favorite stitch, the French Knot adds much character to the Piano Shawl.

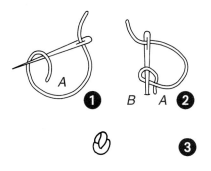

CONTINUOUS FRENCH KNOT—Form the stitch the same as the French Knot, except finish by making a short stitch, and repeat. Work towards the left. Place the stitches farther apart to make Continuous Pistil Stitch.

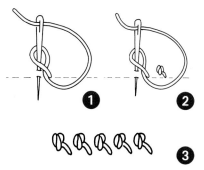

FOUR-LEGGED KNOT STITCH—This is a combination of Cross Stitch and French Knot. Come up at A. 1. Stitch from B to C. 2. Slide the needle under the stitch without piercing the fabric, and loop the thread around the needle. Pull snug, and pull the needle through. 3. Bring the needle down at D.

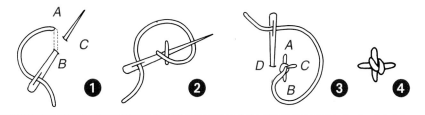

ITALIAN KNOTTED BORDER STITCH—This stitch is actually an elongated Fly Stitch tacked with a French Knot. Come up at A. 1. Stitch from B to C. 2. Form a French Knot. Make the following stitch to the right of the first.

PISTIL STITCH—Form this stitch the same as the French Knot, but sink the thread further away.

HERRINGBONE STITCH. Working towards the right, hold the needle horizontal to the row of stitching, having it pointed towards the previous stitch. 1. Come up at A. At the top of the row, stitch from B to C. 2. At the bottom of the row, stitch from D to E. Repeat 1 and 2.

The Herringbone, along with the Feather Stitch, are two of the most common stitches found on antique crazy quilts, such as on this block. They were treated as utilitarian stitches, most often used to hold patches in place. Collection of the author.

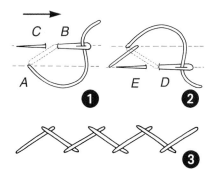

BRETON STITCH–Come up at A, at the bottom of the row. 1. Stitch from B to C. 2. Slide the needle behind the stitch just made without piercing the fabric, and pull through. 3. Stitch from E to D. "E" is at the center line of the following stitch. Repeat steps 1 through 3.

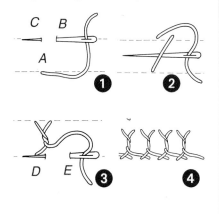

CLOSED HERRINGBONE–Make the same as the Herringbone Stitch, but have the stitches meet at the top and bottom of the row. Another way to form this stitch is to work a row of regular Herringbone, then another over it, staggering the stitches to have the second row worked into the spaces left by the first.

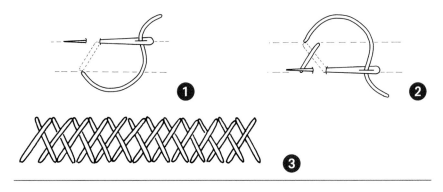

CHEVRON STITCH–Come up at A. 1. With the thread above the needle, stitch from B to C at the top of the row. 2. Stitch from D to E at the bottom of the row keeping the thread above the needle. 3. With the thread below the needle, stitch from F to D. Repeat steps 1 through 3.

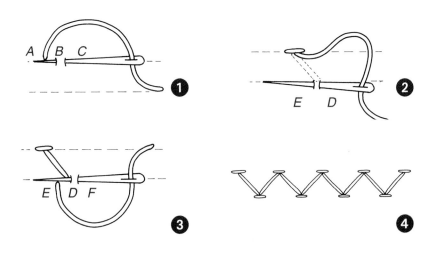

LAZY DAISY STITCH. Come up at A. Stitch from B to C. Finish with a short tacking stitch. This stitch can be varied by using a French Knot, or smaller Lazy Daisy for the tacking stitch, or by making a smaller Lazy Daisy inside a larger one. A Bullion stitch can also be used for the tacking stitch.

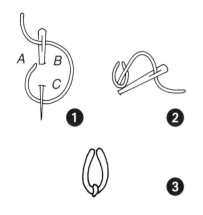

Lazy Daisies almost always seem to have "flower appeal" including here on the Butterstamp Quilt.

DETACHED TWISTED CHAIN–Follow instructions for the Twisted Chain Stitch, but instead of repeating the stitch, finish with two small tacking stitches.

LONG-STEMMED LAZY DAISY STITCH–Make the tacking stitch longer.

BASQUE STITCH–This stitch is worked towards the right. 1. Come up at A, and insert the needle from B to C, do not pull through. 2. Wrap the thread around both ends of the needle as shown, pull snug, and pull through. 3. Insert the needle just beneath the stitch just made, and come up at B. Repeat, forming the following stitch between D and E.

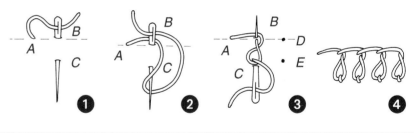

Double Lazy Daisy–Make a short Lazy Daisy, then a larger one outside it. Or, make the smaller stitch inside a larger one.

Kate Greenaway, a turn-of-the-century (1900) artist, drew children in many poses, and these drawings appeared in many crazy quilts worked in Outline Stitch. The embroideries on this quilt are from iron-on transfers published by Dover Publications, Inc. (See Sources).

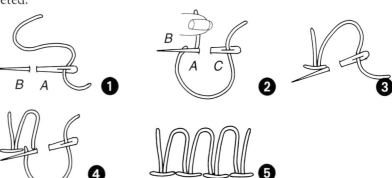

Innovative use of the Outline Stitch, as used on this 1898 crazy quilt. Detail. Collection of the author.

OUTLINE STITCH. Come up at A, and stitch from B to C. Work towards the right, keeping the thread to one side of the needle, and having the needle pointed towards the previous stitch. The stitches form the Backstitch on the reverse of the work. Stitches can also be overlapped slightly to make a wider stitch, or made further apart for a narrower stitch.

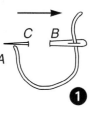

OUTLINE STITCH ROSE—Begin at the center of the rose. Make small Outline Stitches, turning the work for each stitch. Make the stitches longer as the work progresses, making the rose the size desired. You can begin with one color, and change to another to finish. Work the stitches closely so the fabric does not show through the rose.

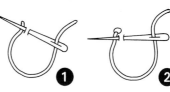

BACKSTITCH—Come up at A, and stitch from B to C. Make the following stitch from C to A, and repeat.

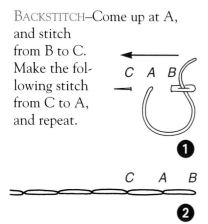

SPLIT STITCH—Work the same as for the Outline Stitch, but run the needle through both fabric and thread for each stitch. This makes a finer outline. The Split Stitch can also be worked as a Backstitch, from right to left, with each stitch piercing the one before it.

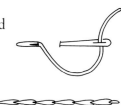

OVERCAST OUTLINE—Work the Outline Stitch and fasten off. Fasten on a second thread. Overcast by sliding the needle under it without piercing the fabric.

TURKEY WORK—Do not fasten the thread to the back of the fabric. 1. Make a short stitch from A to B, pull through, and hold the end with your thumb. Sink the needle at C and come up at A having the thread go under the needle. Make the following stitch to the right of the first. The resulting loops can be trimmed evenly when the stitching is completed.

Useful in landscape quilting, the Running Stitch can be like painting with thread.

RUNNING STITCH. Stitch evenly along a line. Make one stitch at a time, or have several on the needle before pulling through.

HOLBEIN STITCH—Make a line of Running Stitch, having the stitches and the spaces between them of equal size. At the end of the row, fasten on a second thread, and make a return row of Running Stitch filling in the spaces left previously.

SATIN STITCH. Bring the needle up at one side of an area to be covered, and down at the other. Repeat, placing each stitch exactly next to the previous one. This stitch also covers the back of the fabric. To conserve thread, the stitches can be made going down, and then up at one side, and repeating at the other side of the design area. To ensure a neat edge, the design can first be outlined in Backstitch or Outline Stitch, working Satin stitch over this.

BASKET SATIN–This consists of groups of Satin Stitches placed perpendicular to each other.

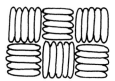

BEETLE STITCH–This is simply the Satin Stitch worked between the same two holes in the fabric. Work enough stitches so they mound up. French knot eyes, straight stitch legs and pistil stitch antennae can be added to form a bug.

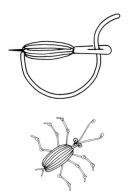

Satin Stitch embroideries make excellent patch decorations. This embroidery is worked from a design in Dover Publications' Traditional Chinese Designs, by Barbara Christopher. The design was transferred using the tissue paper transfer technique.

LACED SATIN STITCH–Work a row of small Satin Stitches spaced evenly. Then, without piercing the fabric, lace a second thread through them.

LONG AND SHORT STITCH–Work the Satin Stitch alternating longer and shorter stitches, to fill in large areas and shade designs.

PADDED SATIN STITCH–Begin by filling the design area with one or more layers of Straight or other stitches. These can also be worked over a small piece of batting for extra loft. Finish with neat, even Satin Stitches to completely cover the padding.

SQUARE STITCH, AND "V" STITCH. These are not stitches as such. They are formed of other stitches such as Straight, Fly, and sometimes Blanket Stitch. Generally, they are made larger and more emphatically than regular stitches, and parts of them are sometimes "tied" with tacking stitches. Found on antique crazy quilts, they may have been an attempt to invent stitches.

Square and "V" stitches are created using Straight and other stitches. There are many variations of these on antique crazy quilts.

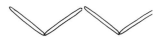

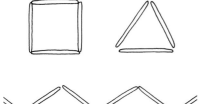

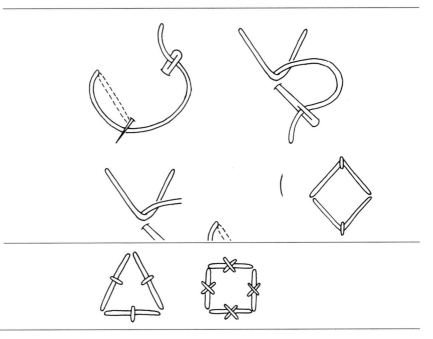

Four-sided Stitch–This stitch consists of Straight or Backstitches to make squares, rectangles, and other geometric shapes. It is easy to work on evenweave fabric.

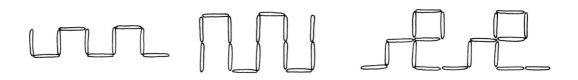

Straight Stitch. Bring the needle up, then down through the fabric. Make stitches in any size desired, placed evenly or randomly.

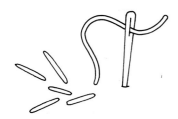

ALGERIAN EYE STITCH—Having all stitches converge at the center, make four stitches vertically and horizontally, followed by four diagonal ones. Add shorter stitches in between the longer ones.

SEED STITCH—this is made by placing two small Straight stitches side by side, and repeating.

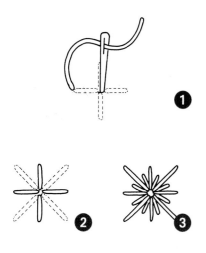

The simplest of stitches, the Straight Stitch has many variations. Antique crazy quilt block is the collection of the author.

ERMINE FILLING STITCH—Make a vertical Straight Stitch followed by two overlapping diagonal ones. Make them in rows to follow a seam, or scatter them randomly.

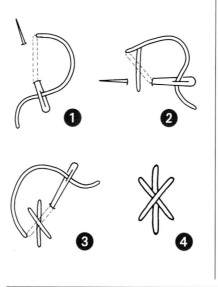

WRAPPED STRAIGHT STITCH—Come up at A, and stitch from B to A. Then pass the needle under the stitch just made without piercing the fabric, and go down at B.

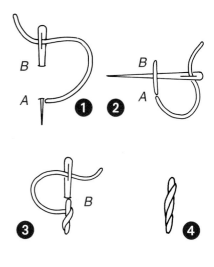

Straight Stitch Fan—All stitches begin at the top of the fan and converge at the base. Fans can be made rounded, tapered, or widened. The number of stitches used can vary from a few to as many as can be fitted.

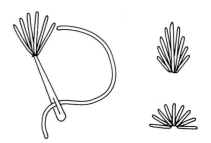

WOVEN AND LACED STITCHES.
Begin by making the base
stitches. Fasten on a second
thread and lace or weave
through them. This thread does
not pierce the fabric except to
begin and end.

DOUBLE-LACED
BACKSTITCH—Begin with a row
of Backstitching. Fasten on a
second thread and pass the needle under each consecutive
stitch. Turn, and lace in the
reverse direction.

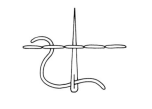

WOVEN SATIN STITCH—Begin by
filling an area with Satin Stitch.
Fasten on a second thread and
weave back and forth until
filled in.

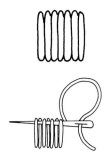

LACED BLANKET STITCHES—Begin with
two rows of evenly spaced Blanket
stitches. Fasten on a second thread and
lace between them as shown.

*Woven roses and fans
worked in wool threads on
the Horses and Roses
Wool Quilt.*

WOVEN ROSE OR
SPIDERWEB STITCH—Begin
with an odd number of
spokes using Fly Stitches
and a Straight Stitch, or
all Straight Stitches meeting at the center. Fasten
on a second thread at the
center; weave over and
under spokes until filled
in.

PEKINESE STITCH—Begin with a row of
Backstitch. Fasten on a second thread,
come up at A, pass needle under first
Backstitch. Skip one Backstitch; bring
needle up under the following stitch,
then down under the skipped stitch having the thread over the needle.
Repeat.

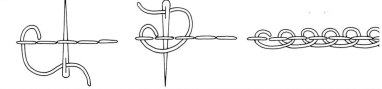

RAISED SPIDERWEB STITCH—Make any number of spokes of Straight
Stitches, overlapping at the center. Fasten on a second thread, come
up at the center and work a backstitch over one spoke and under the
previous two. Repeat, working clockwise.

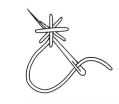

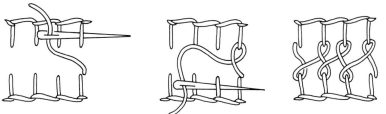

The Stitch Plates

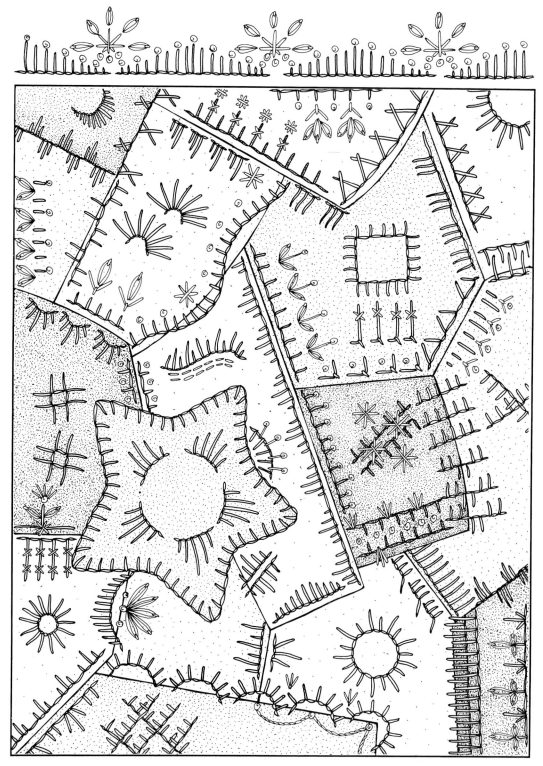

OTHER NEEDLEWORK: Blanket stitch is used to edge wool blankets and clothing, and to apply appliqués. The Buttonhole stitch is used for buttonholes, appliqué, monogramming and other fine embroidery.

OTHER NEEDLEWORK: Bullion knots are used in dimensional embroidery, especially Wool, and Brazilian embroidery which is worked in rayon threads. Try them in silk ribbon!

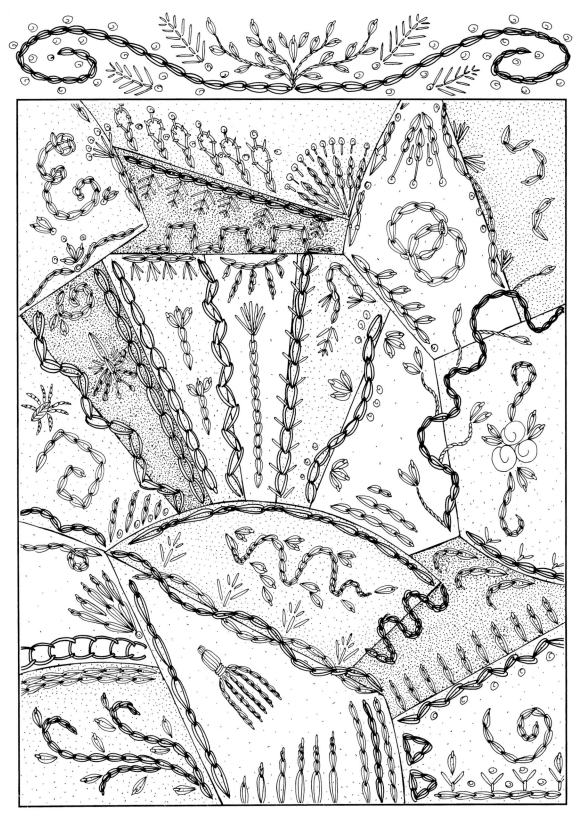

OTHER NEEDLEWORK: Very fine chain stitch worked evenly to form various designs is called "Tambour Work" and was often done using a hook. This was once worked on net or sheer fabric for a lacey effect. Some very beautiful tambour work was done in the late 1700s and early 1800s in the U.S. and Europe to make baby's caps, shawls, collars, and bridal veils.

Chain Stitch is also used for outlining and filler in crewel and other types of embroidery.

OTHER NEEDLEWORK: Excellent in landscape embroideries, the main feature of this stitch is its textural quality. Try it in different thread types and in silk ribbon. This stitch can also be used to couch other threads. Coral Stitch can be worked from left to right by wrapping the thread in the opposite direction.

Plate 5: Couching

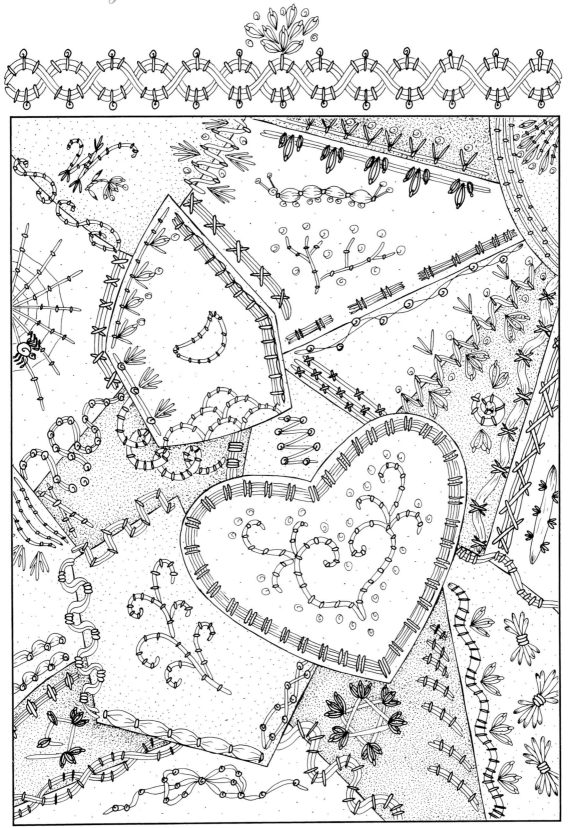

OTHER NEEDLEWORK: Couching was often used in Victorian crazy quilts to fasten on chenille or stranded threads. It is also used in Brazilian embroidery to form fine leaves and branches. In silk and metal embroideries couching is used to secure metal threads that cannot be sewn through fabric. It is also used in silk ribbon embroidery to fasten laid ribbons.

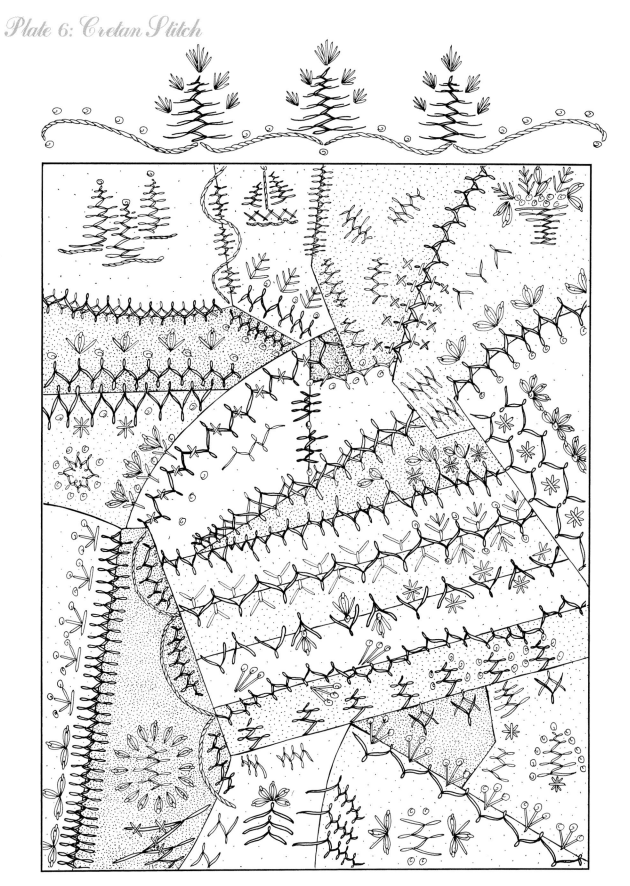

OTHER NEEDLEWORK: The Cretan Stitch is used to make leaves in crewel and other forms of embroidery. The Open Cretan is an extremely versatile crazy quilting stitch, quick to make, and can be "embellished" with additional stitches.

OTHER NEEDLEWORK: Cross stitch is a common form of embroidery worked on Aida cloth or evenweave linen to make pictures, samplers, and many other projects. It can also be worked on plain fabrics using "waste canvas," a lightweight canvas that is basted onto any fabric, embroidered over in cross stitch, then removed by pulling out its individual threads. Double cross stitches made very small appear as dots and are used as filler stitches in crewel embroidery. The 1/2 cross stitch is useful for sewing on beads.

OTHER NEEDLEWORK: A beautiful stitch, and used in many antique crazy quilts, sometimes as the only decorative stitch. This stitch was known as "Coral Stitch" in Victorian times. The Victorian "Feather Stitch" consisted of a straight central line with angled "arms" on one or both sides of the line, identical to a slanted Blanket Stitch.

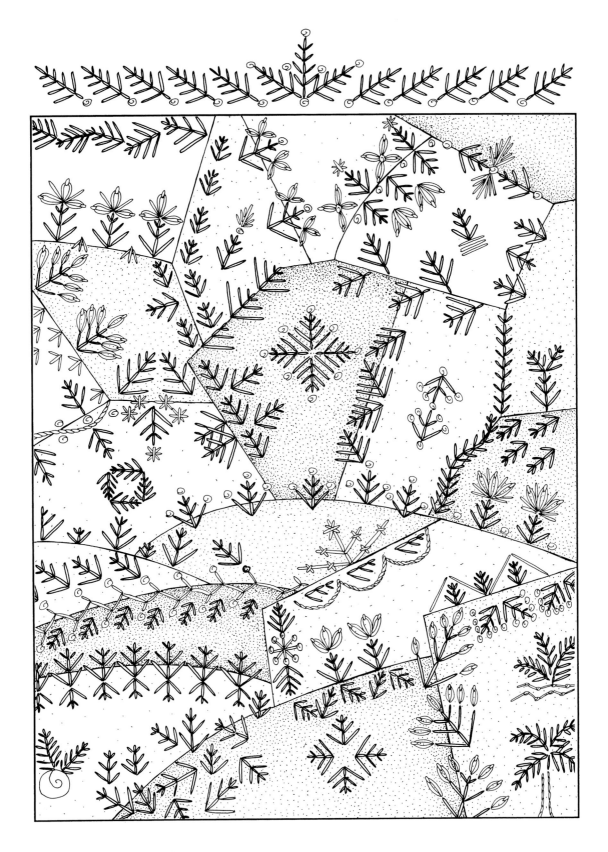

OTHER NEEDLEWORK: This stitch can easily be worked to fit the "grid" of evenweave fabric in cross stitch or needlepoint designs. In silk ribbon embroidery, twist the ribbon to make ferns.

OTHER NEEDLEWORK: The Fishbone stitch defies exact definition. There are several different ways to make the stitch. It can be used to make beautiful leaves in wool, crewel, and other types of embroidery.

OTHER NEEDLEWORK: Among the uses for Fly stitch include its versatility in building up stitch combinations, and its use as a base for a flower or bud. Scatter them for filler stitches.

Plate 12: French Knot

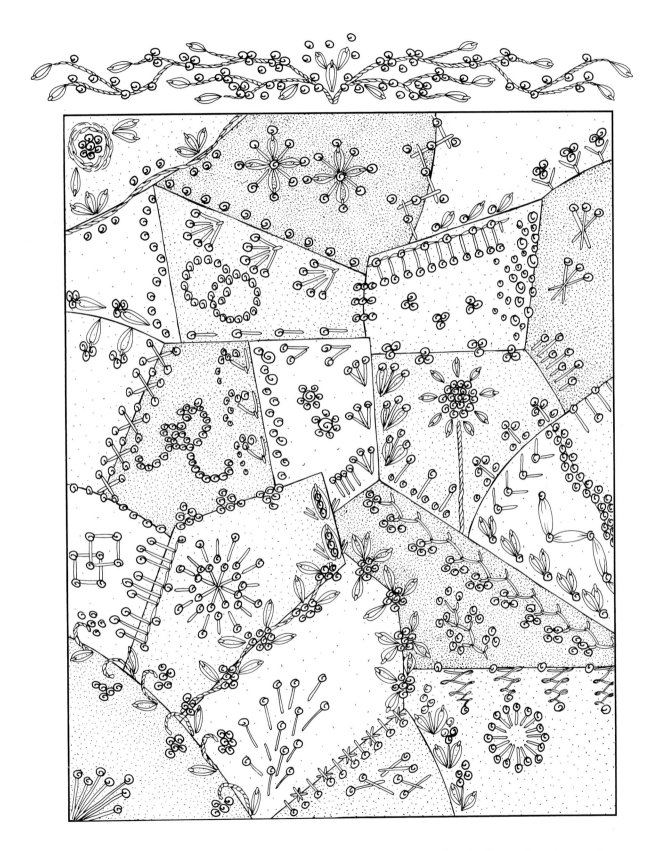

OTHER NEEDLEWORK: The French Knot is used as a filler stitch in crewel and other embroidery, and sometimes in place of Colonial Knot for candlewicking. It can be added to needlepoint and cross stitch. The Pistil Stitch is useful in embroidering flowers.

PART ONE - THE BASICS OF CRAZY QUILTING 71

OTHER NEEDLEWORK: The Herringbone and related stitches are excellent for a base row along crazy quilt patch seams. The Chevron stitch is commonly used in smocking.

OTHER NEEDLEWORK: This stitch is a single version of the Chain stitch, and is sometimes called "Single Chain," or "Detached Chain." The Victorians termed it the "Picot Stitch." This stitch has many uses, from delineating flower petals, to filler stitches in crewel and other embroideries. It can be worked on top of needlepoint for added dimension, and in cross stitch. Very useful in silk ribbon embroidery to form flowers of many types.

OTHER NEEDLEWORK: Also called "Stem Stitch," the Outline is a much-used embroidery stitch. Kate Greenaway's child-characters were outline stitched onto many Victorian crazy quilts. Turkey work is used in dimensional embroidery. Outline Stitch Roses are often used in Wool or Silk Ribbon Embroidery.

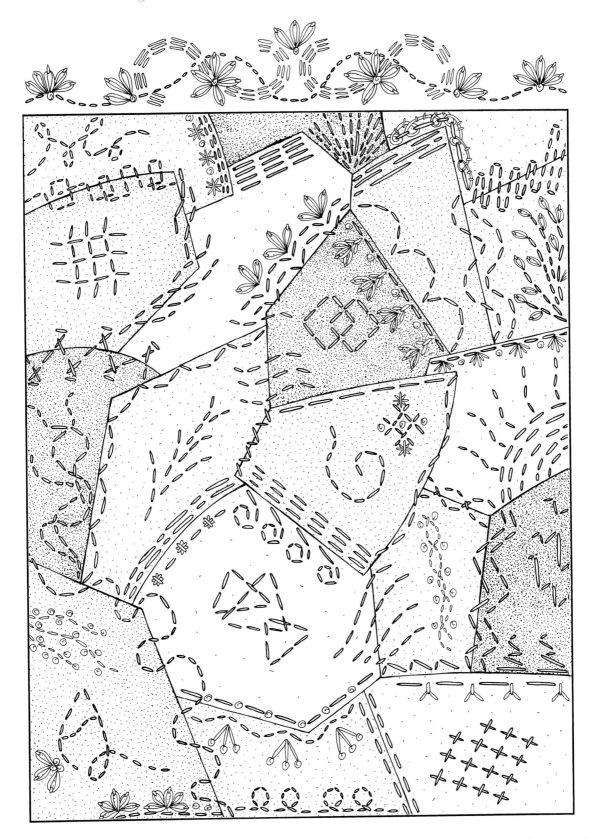

OTHER NEEDLEWORK: Made tiny, and very evenly, this is also the quilting stitch. The same stitch is used for Sashiko, Oriental quilting that is worked in white thread such as a size 8 pearl cotton usually on one layer of indigo-blue fabric. Sashiko is intended to reinforce the fabric rather than quilt layers together. The Holbein Stitch is used in Blackwork.

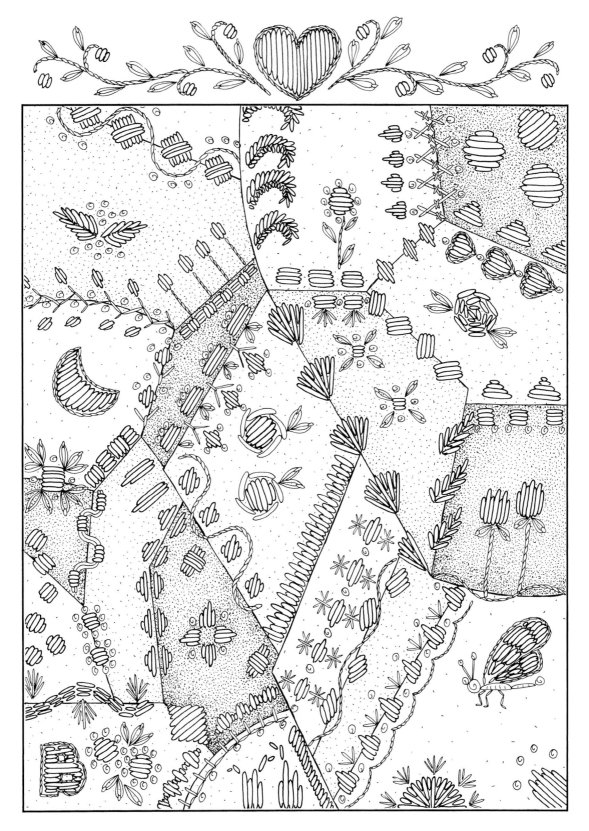

OTHER NEEDLEWORK: Coming from many different embroidery traditions, from most parts of the world, Satin Stitch embroidery is perhaps best known by beautiful and colorful Oriental embroideries worked in lustrous silk threads. Monograms stitched in cotton floss is a western tradition, with many elaborate ones done by the Victorians.

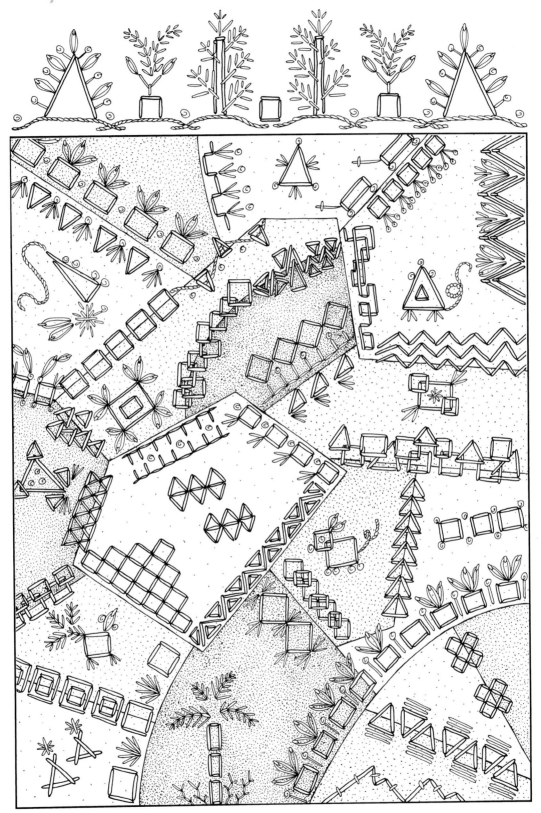

OTHER NEEDLEWORK: These are not stitches as such. They are formed of other stitches such as Straight, Fly, and sometimes Blanket Stitch. Generally, they are made larger and more emphatically than regular stitches, and parts of them are sometimes "tied" with tacking stitches. Found on antique crazy quilts, they may have been an attempt to invent stitches.

OTHER NEEDLEWORK: One of the most versatile of all stitches, the Straight Stitch can be used to form the Fern Stitch, Box and "V," and Fan stitches. Putting a French Knot at the end of one substitutes for the Pistil Stitch. All of these configurations are found in Victorian crazy quilts, and also as filler stitches in crewel and other embroideries. The Algerian Eye Stitch is traditionally found in needlepoint and cross stitch designs.

OTHER NEEDLEWORK: Woven roses are common to wool and silk ribbon embroidery.

The Tissue Paper Transfer Method

I thought I had invented this method, but then found it in Erica Wilson's books on embroidery! In any case, it has been a foolproof way to get designs onto crazy patches without leaving permanent marks on the fabric. It is ideal for almost any small embroidery design. For larger designs, the paper can sometimes disintegrate too quickly, but can still be done if the design is divided into smaller parts.

Trace the design onto tissue paper. I use a hard-lead pencil, making a fine line. If you are doing white on white embroidery, the pencil may come off onto the thread. Do a small sample, then wash it to see whether any pencil remains. If so, experiment with a permanent marker. Do not use a water soluble marker. You can also iron an iron-on transfer design onto the tissue.

The tissue paper transfer method is easy, effective, and leaves no marks on the fabric.

Cut around the drawn design leaving about 1/2-1 inch of excess. Place the fabric in an embroidery hoop, and baste the tissue paper onto the fabric.

Embroider the outlines of the design, then tear away the paper. Continue by filling in the design with embroidery if desired.

Spiders and spiderwebs are favorite subjects for embroidery on crazy quilts, as here on the Ladies and Fans quilt.

Spiders and Webs

Spiders and webs are not the most-used symbol appearing on Victorian crazy quilts as is sometimes thought. Embroidered fans and rings take precedence by far over spiders and webs on the quilts I've seen.

There are many theories regarding the use of spiders and webs in quilting and the needlearts. I prefer the practical reality–the webs catch nasty bugs. They are symbolic of the ecology of summer, a part of nature's balancing act. Nature weaves an intricate web, and we are part of that intricacy, just a patch in the web of life!

It only stands to reason that spiders can be portrayed in as many ways as there are types of them, and there are many. For starters, spiders are shiny or dull, short- or long-legged, small or large, colorful or gray, patterned or plain, luminescent or hairy. Some have eight eyes, others have none. They all have eight legs!

The same goes for webs. Not all are as perfectly shaped as those of the garden spider. To embroider a web, couch metallic, rayon, or silk threads making the long strands, then the shorter ones.

A spider can be made of embroidery stitches as shown here, or by combining several sizes of beads.

Make two or more French Knots for the head.
Double cross stitch (Star stitch), or a Double Lazy Daisy for the middle.
Padded Satin (Beetle stitch), or Double Lazy Daisy for the end.
Make legs of Coral or Straight Stitches.

Artful Embellishments

It is artful embellishment that distinguishes the most fanciful of both antique and modern crazy quilts. Satin-stitched monograms interlaced with embroidered flowers, charming Kate Greenaway outlined figures, ribbons fashioned into flowers, and sewn-on beads, buttons, and tassels are some sewn methods. Others include painting, stenciling, and transferring photos onto fabric. In addition to the fancy stitches worked along patch edges, embellishments add dimension, color, texture, and variety to the "crazed china" surface of crazy patching. All of these additions can enliven a quilt by taking its surface beyond the ordinary, explaining why crazy quilts are sometimes referred to as "art quilts".

Like works of art, from simple to complex, a crazy quilt is the unique expression of its maker. Sometimes it doesn't take much. Simple techniques can be extraordinary in their effect, from fastening on a piece of old lace with a particular embroidery stitch, to discovering a fabulous new way to sew a scrap of fabric into the shape of a flower. The individual touches that each pair of hands, like handwriting, bring to a quilt-in-progress are often enough to put a stamp of personality on it.

Sometimes a unique choice of technique can make a difference. Pieces of needlepoint and cross stitch are not the norm for crazy quilt decor, and yet the Wool Quilt demonstrates the efficacy of these as decorative patches. Do you have pieces of unfinished needlework hidden away in a closet or the attic that could be made into crazy patches? Consider making a quilt displaying your favorite of the arts or needlearts, or one that uses up unfinished projects.

We may think of stenciling and other types of printing as being for paper and walls, but they can also be done on fabric, as shown by the Butterstamp quilt.

Try the techniques in both parts of this chapter, experimenting on scraps of fabric and saving them to use later as patches. Is it backwards to embellish the patches before patching the quilt? Not at all! The Victorian

A highly embellished crazy quilt features a central panel with ribbon roses. Other embellishment on this quilt includes painting on silk, cotton and silk floss and chenille embroideries. Courtesy of The Kirk Collection, Omaha, NE. Photo by Nancy T. Kirk.

A needlepoint design by Anne Orr, from Full-Color Charted Designs, published by Dover Publications, Inc., 1984. Anne Orr was a designer of needlework during the early 1900s. This is stitched of silk ribbons, wool, silk, and rayon threads, then used as a patch on the Horses and Roses Wool Quilt.

memories quilt was made exactly this way. Far less than perfect, the trial pieces could easily have been thrown out. Instead, they were tossed into a basket, out of which the quilt was patched. This quilt went together quickly with most of its embellishment already finished.

The two parts to this chapter include the applied techniques of ribbonwork, appliqué, dimensional and other embroidery, fabric manipulation, and using beads and buttons in the first. The second features methods that become intrinsic to the fabric, such as dyeing, painting, rubbings, stenciling, and photo transfer.

Learning New Techniques

If you haven't done them before, most of these techniques can be learned easily. But with some, like punchneedle embroidery, you will be lucky to make perfect stitches on the first try. Try, then try again, perhaps with different fabric or thread.

It is very true that challenging things become easy once learned (do you recall learning how to drive!?), and that success happens more easily with an "I can do it" attitude. Indeed, Queen Victoria in this instance may have been likely to recommend that you have the courage of your convictions!

Part 1: Embroidered and Sewn Techniques

Silk Ribbon Embroidery

NEEDED:

chenille needle size 18, scissors, 4" embroidery hoop, silk ribbons.

One of the many needle arts practiced by Victorian ladies, silk ribbon embroidery is romantic in its appeal, easy to do, and a "must try" if you haven't already! The basic embroidery stitches are used, with silk ribbons in place of threads or floss. The commonest subjects are flowers, with the stitches dimensionally portraying flower parts. A ribbon stitch becomes a leaf or petal, a French knot makes a flower center, or a lazy daisy

Working silk ribbon embroidery using 4mm silk ribbon. In the basket are 4mm and 7mm ribbons, the most common widths used.

stitch a bud, and so on.

Combining these floral stitches into bouquets and other florals, and cottage garden scenes is easy to do and makes beautiful focal points on a crazy quilt. Just as effective is peppering a quilt top with individual silk flowers randomly placed.

Silk has a weightless, airy quality, imparting a painterly characteristic to this needle art, a trait enhanced by using hand-dyed or dye-painted ribbons. Variegated silk ribbons can be purchased, or you can easily dye them yourself. Infinite shade progressions, multi-colorations, and other effects are easy to achieve, and can make your floral embroideries appear almost real. Some of these dye techniques appear in part 2 of this chapter.

Silk embroidery ribbons from Japan, sold under several different brand names, are firmly woven of filament silk for embroidery use. They come in widths of 2mm, 4mm, 7mm, and wider. The 4mm width is available in the widest color range, and is the most common width for embroidery.

Another excellent embroidery ribbon from Japan, a 4mm silk-like synthetic, is available in about 100 colors. Made of a milk-protein based fiber sometimes called "azlon," it is sold under different brand names. This ribbon is lighter in weight than either polyester or rayon, and is washable and colorfast.

There are many other types of ribbons available, of fibers including rayon, nylon, polyester, metallics, and others that are either woven, braided, or knitted. You may want to experiment with some of them for the special effects that can be added to silk ribbon work.

How to Thread the Needle

This technique will keep the silk ribbon secure in the needle while allowing most of its length to be used. Place one end of the ribbon through the eye of the needle, then run the needle through the ribbon, about 1/4 inch from the same end. Pull on the long end of the ribbon to settle the "knot" into place.

To begin, make a tiny stitch on the back of the fabric, then run the needle through the tail of the stitch. OR, leave a tail on the back and work the first stitch through it to secure. Knotting the ribbon should not be done. The needle can hang up on the knots if you happen to stitch into them.

Silk ribbon was used in combination with Size 12 Pearl Cotton to embroider these moss roses on the Victorian quilt.

Tips for Silk Ribbon Embroidery

❶ Use short lengths of ribbon, about 12-14 inches. Longer ribbons may begin to wear and fray at the edges.

❷ Use a size 18 Chenille needle when stitching with 4mm and 7mm ribbons. This size needle makes a hole in the fabric that is large enough for the ribbon to slide through easily, reducing wear on the ribbon.

❸ A small, 3-inch or 4-inch embroidery hoop is recommended in order to keep the fabric from being buckled, and is small enough that your fingers can reach the stitches.

❹ Choose embroidery ribbons that are high quality. Those from Japan tend to be smooth and tightly woven, holding up well to embroidery.

❺ Make the stitches loosely, observing each as it forms, and stopping before the ribbon is pulled too tightly.

❻ Allow the ribbon to untwist between stitches. When making Ribbon and Straight stitches, lay the ribbon onto the surface of the fabric, and hold it with your thumb while pulling the needle through.

❼ Ironing the ribbons before embroidering can give a little extra body to them.

❽ To press the finished embroidery, place it face down on a towel-covered ironing board, and press lightly with a dry iron. Take care not to squash the embroidery, and do not use steam.

Ways to Vary Silk Ribbon Stitches

Stack one stitch directly on top of a previous one. Leaves of Ribbon stitch can be enhanced with a second shade of green in a slightly smaller stitch made on top of the first.

Combine one type of stitch with another, such as French Knots in the centers of Lazy Daisy Stitch.

Twist the ribbon before making a stitch. Straight, Ribbon, and Outline stitches can be twisted once or many times for different effects.

Stitches for Silk Ribbon Embroidery

STRAIGHT STITCH

This corner block detail shows silk ribbon embroidered daisy petals. Collection of Rocky Mountain Quilts, York Village, Maine.

Come up through the fabric at A, then down at B to make one stitch.

This is a simple, but very useful stitch. Group them for flowers, or use them for leaves.

TWISTED STRAIGHT STITCH

Same as the Straight Stitch, but twist the ribbon before going down at B. The ribbon can be loosely or tightly twisted.

Use these for narrow flower petals, leaves, grass, and ferns.

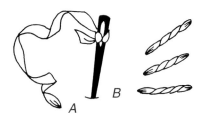

JAPANESE RIBBON STITCH

Smooth the ribbon onto the surface of the fabric, then pierce the end of the stitch and pull through. A variation is to allow the ribbon between A and B to "pouf," making a slightly rounded stitch.

Excellent for leaves and flower petals. Make clusters of them for tree tops.

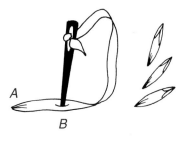

OUTLINE STITCH
TWISTED OUTLINE STITCH

Keep the ribbon to one side of the needle while stitching. Make the stitches shorter to negotiate curves.

Use plain or twisted in straight or curved lines for flower stems, tree trunks, and outlining. Use thread instead of ribbon for very fine stems.

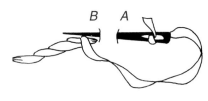

OUTLINE STITCH ROSE

Work the Outline Stitch in a circular fashion, beginning from the center and working outwards. This Rose can also be started around a cluster of French Knots.

LAZY DAISY STITCH
LONG-STEM LAZY DAISY STITCH

The needle passes over the ribbon for the first part of the stitch. A short tacking stitch secures it. A lengthened tacking stitch creates a long-stem stitch.

Use one stitch for a rosebud or a leaf, or group them for flowers.

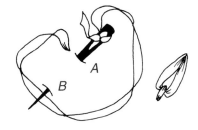

CHAIN STITCH ROSE

Beginning at the center, work Chain Stitch in a circular fashion. This Rose can be started with a French Knot center.

PIERCED LOOP STITCH

Keeping ribbon smooth, pierce ribbon near to A, then pull through, stopping when the loop is the size desired. In a motif, work these last so other stitches won't pull them out.

Make Loop Stitch flowers, and use as filler stitches in florals. French Knots can be used to secure them.

FLY STITCH
LONG-STEM FLY STITCH

Stitch from B to C, with the needle passing over the ribbon. A short tacking stitch secures the stitch. A longer tacking stitch creates a long-stem Fly Stitch.

Use for flower calyxes, or turn upside-down and stack them for Foxglove. Continue the tacking stitch into Twisted Outline Stitch for a stem.

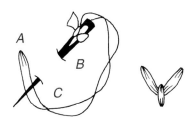

FEATHER STITCH
DOUBLE FEATHER STITCH

Take a stitch first from one side, then the other of an imaginary line. To work the Double Feather Stitch, take two stitches on each side of the line.

Very useful for foliage, shrubbery, and filler in florals.

FERN STITCH

Make these as groupings of three Straight Stitches, or one Straight followed by Fly Stitches. Twist the ribbon for a finer stitch.

Add ferns to cottage garden and other florals.

FRENCH KNOT
PISTIL STITCH

Wrap the ribbon one or more times around the needle, pull snug, then bring the needle through. Wrap very loosely once, or several times for a larger, rose-like knot.

Use for Queen Anne's Lace, Lilacs, and filler stitches.

The Pistil Stitch is a variation of the French Knot. Wrap around the needle, then sink the needle farther from the beginning of the stitch.

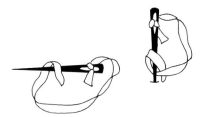

Weaving

Keeping the ribbon smooth, make long Straight Stitches horizontally. Then make vertical stitches while weaving through the horizontal ones.

Use weaving for baskets and to fill in hearts and other objects.

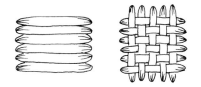

WOVEN ROSE

Make 5 spokes using ribbon or thread. Starting from the center, weave around until the spokes are filled.

COUCHING

Thread two needles with matching or contrasting ribbons. Fasten on the first ribbon and bring the needle through to the front of the fabric. Fasten on the second ribbon, and make French Knots or small Straight Stitches to hold the first ribbon in place. Fasten off both when finished.

Couched streamers and bows are elegant additions to floral embroideries.

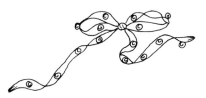

Creating a Rose Motif

Although roses are used here, many other flowers may be represented instead.

❶ Begin with several Outline, Woven, or Chain Stitch roses to establish the placement of the design. Motifs can be made to fit into spaces such as corners and borders by placing these elements appropriately. Add leaves of Lazy Daisy or Ribbon stitches.
❷ Work Feather or Fern Stitches to begin the background. Add several Rosebuds, each consisting of a Lazy Daisy with a Fly Stitch.

❸ Add Twisted Straight Stitch flowers, and finish by scattering French Knots throughout.

Designs for Silk Ribbon Embroidery

These designs can be worked freehand. If you prefer to follow markings, place dots on the fabric using a tailor's chalk pencil, and place the stitches according to the markings.

Detail of a cottage garden scene worked in soft shades of hand-dyed ribbons on a dark green background fabric from Green Mountain Hand-dyed Linens.

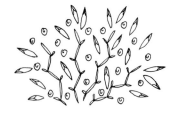

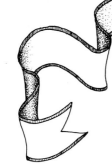

Ribbonwork

NEEDED:

scissors, pins, sewing thread and needles, ribbons.

Manipulating ribbons offers a possibility of greater dimensionality than most other embellishment methods. Dramatic-looking flowers crafted of luxurious, wide ribbons can make a bold statement on a crazy quilt.

How to use ribbonwork depends on the result you wish to achieve. One flower with a leaf creates an attractive singular detail, while floral bouquets, sprays, and other arrangements can spread out over a patch or more, even becoming the focus of the quilt. Lengths of ribbon embroidered or couched along patch seams can take the place of embroidery. Used in combination, bolder ribbonwork flowers are soft-

ened by the more delicate touches of silk ribbon and other types of embroidery.

Wired, soft rayon, and other ribbons for ribbonwork.

Ribbons for Ribbonwork

Woven ribbons of many fibers and widths are found in sewing, craft, and bridal shops. Be sure to select fabric ribbons for sewing and needlearts, rather than "craft" ribbons. They should be made of fabric that is wash- or dry-cleanable.

Most ribbons can be gathered, folded, scrunched, couched, and some of the narrow ones can be sewn through fabric. Most ribbon types are available in several widths.

Nylon Organdy Ribbons are sheer, appearing soft and shadowy on a quilt's surface. The narrow ones can be sewn through fabric. Form them into accordion roses and gathered flowers, and couch them across patches.

Satin Ribbons are either single or double face. Double-face ribbons have the satin finish on both sides, with single face one side only. Satin is a weave, not a fiber, so these ribbons can be found made of acetate, polyester, silk, or other fibers.

Many satin ribbons are firmly woven, making them suitable for flowers and trims that resist flattening. Some of the imported ones are wide, soft, and have wired edges for making shaped flowers.

Silk embroidery ribbons wider than 7mm make lovely soft flowers. Plain weave silk ribbons are available with finished, or unfinished edges.

Bias-cut, raw edged silk ribbons in attractive variegated shades are ideal for many creative uses, such as embellishment of wall quilts. To use them in functional quilts, their raw edges should be concealed or finished in some way.

Rayon or acetate ribbons from France with wired edges, available in several widths make beautiful flowers. Some of these have ombre shading. The wire can be used to gather the ribbon. For a tighter gather, remove the wire and run a gathering thread instead.

Another type of rayon ribbon, from Japan, is soft and loosely woven. About 1/2-inch wide, it can be sewn through fabric, or used to make soft folded or gathered flowers.

Novelty ribbons made of metallics, velvets, printed fabrics, and ribbons with various edge treatments can also be found. As with other ribbons and trims, be sure they are suitable for the project.

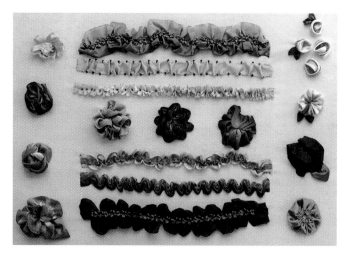

A display of ribbonwork flowers and trims.

Ribbon Trims and Flowers

Experiment with a variety of ribbon types and widths in making the trims and flowers on these pages. Although some are better suited to wide or narrow ribbons, most can be made of many widths.

The length of ribbon to use in making flowers depends on the type of flower and how full you want to make it. For instance, a 2-inch wide ribbon will require a greater length than one that is 1/2 inch in width, to make a gathered 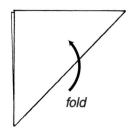 flower of equal fullness.

Sew leaves on along with, or before the flowers. French Knots can be added to the centers of flowers, and some flowers can be turned on their sides for side- and three- quarter views.

Cutting bias ribbons.

You can make your own bias ribbons by cutting silk or other lightweight fabrics into strips.

❶ Begin with a square of fabric.

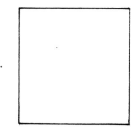

❷ Fold the fabric diagonally as shown.

fold

❸ Press a crease along the fold, then cut along it. Measure, and cut strips as needed.

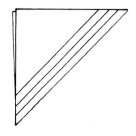

Fold the bias strips lengthwise, and use them to make gathered flowers. Or, sew the strips into tubes, turn the tubes right side out, and press them flat. Ruche or fold these into flowers the same as for ribbons.

Couched Ribbon Trim

Make this trim directly on a crazy patch. Use it in place of the embroidery along patch edges, or lay it across patches, either straight or meandering.

Secure both ends of the ribbon under patch seams, then work embroidery stitches along the ribbon.

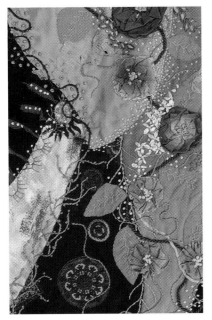

Organdy ribbons wind their way across patches, some couched with French Knots of silk ribbon. Gathered ribbon flowers with appliquéd leaves spill diagonally across the Piano Shawl, interspersed with delicate silk ribbon flo-

Scrunched and Couched Ribbon

Begin by securing one end under a seam, then couch the ribbon while scrunching it. This is easy to do. Make a stitch, such as a French Knot, push the ribbon towards the stitch, and place the following stitch to hold the "scrunch" in place. You can also pin the scrunches, then couch.

Gathered Trims

Velvet ribbons can be shaped and stuffed as demonstrated by this antique velvet pillow. Collection of Rocky Mountain Quilts, York Village, Maine.

Begin with a length of ribbon about twice as long as the finished trim will be.

With matching thread, baste along one or both edges, or along the center of the ribbon. To ruche a ribbon, work basting along it in a zig zag fashion. Pull up the stitches to gather the trim.

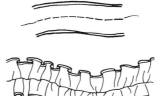

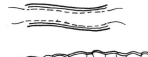

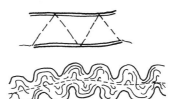

Arrange a gathered trim straight or meandering across a patch. Tuck the ends under

patch edges. Hand-sew or embroider along the trim to secure it into place.

Gathered ribbon trims can also be couched with beads, buttons, and silk ribbon embroidery.

Gathered Flowers

The length of ribbon to use for gathered flowers depends on how full you want the flower to be. A lightly gathered flower will look differently than a very full one made with a longer piece of ribbon. Experiment with various lengths.

❶ Circle Flower. Sew the long ends of a length of ribbon together, then run a gathering thread along one edge. Pull up tightly, and fasten off. Shape the flower while tacking it down.

For a variation of this, use two ribbons of different widths and/or colors held together as one.

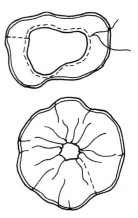

❷ Winding Flower. Edge-gather or ruche a length of ribbon. Sew one end of the ribbon to a crazy quilt patch, then wind the remainder of it around while stitching it down.

3 Double Flower. Following instructions for the Circle or Winding Flower, gather the ribbon along its center. Stitch the gathered line to a crazy quilt patch, folding the two edges upwards to form a double row of petals.

4 Berries and Buds. Sew a short length of ribbon into a circle, then gather both long edges. Sew one or both of the gathered edges to the background fabric. These can be used for buds, berries, and some flower types. A pinch of stuffing can be added inside the berry or flower.

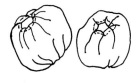

Folded Flowers and Leaf

Accordion Rose

1 Thread a needle with matching thread and set it aside. Begin at the center of a length of ribbon, using about 9 inches of 3/8-inch ribbon, or 12 inches of 3/4-inch ribbon. Fold the left end of the ribbon down.

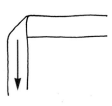

2 Fold the same end upwards and to the back.

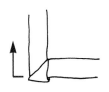

3 Fold the right end backwards. Continue to fold, alternating ends and always folding backwards.

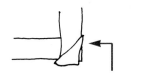

To end, hold the final fold firmly, let go of the previous folds and slowly pull one end downwards. Stop pulling as soon as the rose forms.

Secure by stitching through the base, then the center of the flower. Trim the ends of the ribbon off, and stitch the rose to a crazy patch.

Prairie Point Leaf

The finished size of the leaf depends on the ribbon's width. Fold, and run a gathering thread as shown. Pull up to gather, fasten off, and trim the ends. Stitch the leaf to a crazy patch, placing a flower over the gathered end.

Tea Rose or Rosebud

A large rosebud can be made of a 14-inch length of 1 1/2-inch-wide ribbon.

Thread a needle with matching thread and set it aside. Remove the wire from the lower edge of the ribbon if it is a wired ribbon.

1 Fold one end downwards, then wrap the long end of the ribbon loosely around the fold, finishing by folding the end downwards.

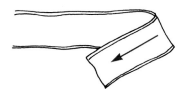

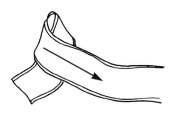

2 Sew through the base several times, then wrap the thread around it several times and fasten off. Trim the ribbon ends close to the stitching.

Fold the lowest petal downwards to conceal the stitching, and sew the rosebud to a patch. Arrange the petals and tack them in place with a few stitches.

Using Crinoline in Ribbonwork

Ribbon flowers can be tacked onto crinoline, a stiffened fabric, as they are made.

Although the crazy patch with its underlying foundation is often a sufficient base, crinoline can be used to provide extra stability to a grouping of flowers. The crinoline is trimmed close to the stitching before it is tacked onto a project.

If crinoline is placed in contact with silks and other fine fabrics, it could saw into the fibers of these fabrics. To prevent this, stitch a piece of fabric over the crinoline before it is tacked on.

Ribbon Flowers and Yo-Yos

Winding Rose.

This is made directly on the crazy quilt patch. Secure one end of the ribbon by putting a needle through it. Make sure the needle is of sufficient length to accommodate the windings. Wind the ribbon around the needle until the flower is as full as you want it. Tuck in the end of the ribbon, thread a second needle, and stitch the "petals" in place.

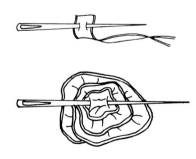

Looped Ribbon Flowers.

Use 1/4-inch satin, or 4mm or 7mm silk ribbon for these. They can be made in hand, or directly on a patch. Holding the

center of the flower, fold the ribbon into loops, one loop at a time. Securely sew the loops at the center to keep all of the petals in place. A small gathered flower added to the center will conceal the stitching.

Yo-Yos.

Yo-yos make lovely flowers, as shown on this detail of the Ladies and Fans quilt.

These are made of fabric, not ribbon, but are included here because they make wonderful flowers. Cut a 4-inch circle of fabric—silk jacquards are an excellent choice! Fold the outer edge under about 1/4 inch, and baste close to this edge. Pull up to gather, and fasten off. Slipstitch the yo-yo to a patch with the opening facing upwards.

Yo-yos can be arranged in side and three-quarter views as well as full-face. French Knots can be added inside the opening. Cut smaller, or larger circles to make flowers of other sizes.

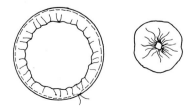

Bias Ribbon Flowers

Ribbon Flower Petals.

Make 4 to 12 petals, depending on the desired fullness of the finished flower. Using wide ribbon or bias scraps of fabric, cut two 2-inch x 3-inch pieces.

❶ Place the two pieces right sides together, and sew as shown. Trim the seam, turn and press the petal. Repeat for the remaining petals.

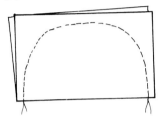

❷ One at a time, baste along the base and pull the thread to gather, then fasten off.

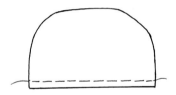

❸ Sew the petals to each other, adding one at a time. Sew the flower onto a crazy patch along with a leaf or two. Take several stitches down through the center of the flower to secure it in place.

Bias Ribbon Rolled Rose.

Thread a needle with matching thread and set it aside. Using about a 6" length of wide ribbon, fold it in two along the center. Roll the folded ribbon 2 or 3 times around the tip of your index finger, having both ends folded downwards so raw edges will be concealed.

fold

Slide the rose off your finger, holding it firmly. Stitch through the base, then wrap the thread around several times and fasten off. Trim close to the thread.

Open out the rose and slipstitch the outer petals to a patch. Then make several stitches down through the center of the rose.

wrap

trim

Wool Embroidery

NEEDED:

wool threads, scissors, embroidery hoop, chenille needles.

Recently popularized by needleworkers from Australia and other parts of the world who have done some beautiful designs with it, wool embroidery is now working its way into the U.S. It is not the crewel embroidery we once associated with wool work. Easy to learn, adaptable to many uses, quick to do, and dimensional, it shares many of the characteristics of silk ribbon embroidery. And, like silk ribbon, it is most often used to depict florals, with stitches forming flower parts and leaves.

Wool embroidery is wonderful for embellishing wool and other crazy quilts, worked along seams or on the centers of patches. As a free form technique, flowers and leaves are easily combined into bouquets, sprays, and other configurations.

Wool embroidery is worked on patches and along seams of this wool quilt.

Threads for Wool Embroidery

Use tapestry, persian, and other wool threads made for embroidery. One strand of DMC® Broder Medici produces a very fine stitch. The heavier Paternayan® Persian was used for most of the fancy stitching in the Wool Quilt. Impressions®, from The Caron Collection, is a 50/50 percent wool/silk thread that embroiders like a dream.

Many other types of threads such as silks, cottons, and rayons can also be used for the wool embroidery stitches and motifs.

Tips and Techniques for Wool Embroidery

1 Use a chenille needle that is large enough to make a hole in the fabric for the wool to pass through easily.

2 When working through two layers of fabric, pull the thread all the way through to form each part of a stitch. This reduces wear on the thread.

3 Begin and end by making 2 or 3 tiny stitches on the back of the piece. No knots, please!

4 If you plan to work florals on the centers of patches, it is often easier to do them before the quilt is patched.

5 Learn the Bullion Stitch if you haven't already. It is a common stitch in wool embroidery, and invaluable for its dimensionality and versatility.

Floral Stitches for Wool Embroidery

The sizes of stitches will vary according to the thickness of the thread used, and, for some, the number of times the thread is wrapped around the needle, such as the French Knot and Bullion Stitch.

Many other stitches can also be used. See the preceding chapter, Victorian Stitches, for more stitches, and stitch instructions.

Real flowers, garden and seed catalogs, and gardening magazines are sources of ideas for additional flowers and motifs. I look forward to January when the gardening catalogs arrive, some of their beautiful illustrations invariably inspiring many ideas for flowers and motifs to adapt for embroidery.

Bullion Stitch Roses and Flowers.

Work overlapping Bullion Stitches around a center of two shorter Bullion stitches, French Knots, or padded Satin Stitch. Add various embroidery stitches to the Bullion stitch to make other types of flowers.

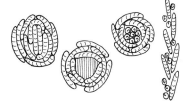

Blanket Stitch Flowers.

Make large, rounded flowers by working Blanket Stitch in a circular fashion. This is easiest to do by first drawing the outer circle of the flower onto the fabric with tailor's chalk. French Knots or Pistil Stitches are used for flower centers.

Straight Stitch Flowers.

Groupings of Straight Stitches make different flower forms. Additional embroidery stitches are added to some.

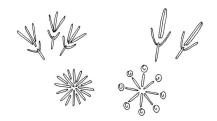

Lazy Daisy Flowers.

Lazy Daisy Stitches make pretty flowers and petals. Add additional embroidery stitches for flower centers and calyxes.

French Knot Flowers.

Lilacs, Wisteria, Queen Anne's Lace, Lupine, and other flowers can be represented by

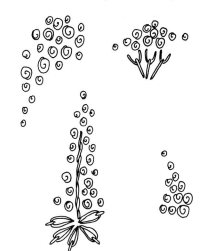

groupings of French Knots. For more natural-looking flowers, vary the sizes of stitches by the number of times the thread is wound around the needle, and by winding the thread loosely for some and tightly for others.

Star Stitch Flowers.

Star Stitch flowers, made very small will appear as dots, and are useful for centers or small flowers.

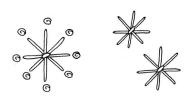

Stitches for Leaves.

Some stitches that can be used for leaves include: 1. The Fishbone Stitch–these are beautiful in a variegated thread, 2. Feather Stitch, 3. Straight Stitches, 4. Fern Stitch, and 5. stacked Lazy Daisy Stitches.

Stems and Branches.

Use Backstitch, Couching, or Outline Stitch for stems and branches.

Weaving.

Weave baskets, vases, and flower centers.

Designs for Wool Embroidery

Wool stitches can be combined into corner motifs, garlands, sprays, baskets, and other shapes. Here are some examples of motifs.

Punchneedle Embroidery

NEEDED:

punch needles, scissors, embroidery hoop, threads, transferred design.

Punchneedle embroidery creates a rug-like pile on the surface of the fabric. It can be worked on any type of crazy quilt, whether wool, silk, or cotton, and in as many types of thread. It can be used to form a solid mat of sheared or looped pile, or to add random looping to other types of embroidery.

Punchneedle is worked on the wrong side of the fabric using a special hollow needle. As the needle is punched through fabric and withdrawn, a loop is formed on the right side.

Punch needles are available in several sizes for different fibers to be used, from crewel yarn to a single strand of embroidery floss. The term, "Russian punch-needle" refers to the finest needle which is used with one strand of silk or cotton floss. Some needles allow the length of the loop to be adjusted.

Above: A fruit tree in full bloom is worked in outline stitch and punch-needle embroidery.

Left: Soft and fuzzy creatures are likely subjects for punchneedle embroidery. Here, a chick is worked on the Horses and Roses quilt.

Threads and Fabrics for Punch Embroidery

Most wool, cotton pearls and flosses, and silk threads work well. Some rayons may be too slippery to hold in the fabric, and metallics can be too coarse to slide through the needle. Following the instructions that came with your needles, experiment with a variety of fibers, using the correct needle size for each. The thread must slide through the eye of the needle easily, but yet not be too loose.

The weave of the background fabric holds the loops in place. Firmly woven linen, cotton, and wool fabrics, and cotton velveteen are excellent choices. Other fabrics such as lightweight silks may be used if they are backed with foundation fabric.

The best designs consist of shapes to be filled in. To fill in large areas, use shading to prevent a "paint by number" look. Also avoid outlining a design in one color and filling in with another, the "coloring book" effect.

Variegated threads are wonderful for punchneedle designs, eliminating the need to change colors for shading. These can be used to achieve natural-looking flowers and trees.

Instructions for Punchneedle Embroidery

1 Draw or transfer a design onto the wrong side of the fabric. Use chalk pencil, an iron-on transfer, or a marking pen intended for needlework.

2 Wrong side up, snugly fit the fabric into an embroidery hoop. Some instructions call for having the fabric "drum-tight." However, I've worked punchneedle with no hoop at all if it is worked into a firm fabric base. To do this, the fabric must be held firmly while punching.

3 To thread the punchneedle, bring the thread down through the shaft, then thread the eye. Hold the needle with the opening facing upwards, or away from yourself. The needle can be held vertically, or at a bit of a slant to prevent working into previously made loops.

4 Keep the tip of the needle in contact with the fabric between punches, sliding it along the surface of the fabric instead of lifting it. Get into a punch-slide rhythm as you work. Trim thread ends close to the surface of the piece.

Tips for Punch Embroidery

Watch that the thread is not hindered, so it can move freely through the needle.

When filling in solid areas, work from side to side: left to right, then right to left, moving away from yourself.

One way to ensure a neat edge is to work Outline Stitch around a design before punching. Outine Stitch worked on the back will appear as backstitch on the front of the fabric.

Areas can be punched a second time to fill them in more completely, or to add a second shade or fiber.

If possible, wash the piece afterwards This helps to secure the loops into the weave of the fabric.

Appliqué

NEEDED:

scissors, size 12 "Sharp" needle, silk pins, beeswax, cotton or silk sewing thread, tightly woven fabric scraps, dry iron and spray bottle. Optional: freezer paper.

Appliqué is the application of one fabric onto another. In crazy quilting, it is most effective used as part of a design with embroidered details added. For instance, a bowl or basket shape is first appliquéd, then filled with embroidered flowers.

The best fabrics are light to medium-weight types that hold a crease easily, and fray minimally. Tightly woven cottons, silks, rayon or wool challis, and taffeta are some examples.

Bold, squared, or rounded shapes are easiest to appliqué. To make narrow strips, use bias cut strips of fabric, pressing the raw edges under.

How to Appliqué

1 Cut out the shape, adding a 1/8 to 1/4-inch seam allowance. Clip inside curves almost to the seam allowance. With a dry iron, press the seam allowance under. If steam is needed to hold a crease, lightly spritz the ironing board with water, then press. Pin or baste the appliqué to the ground fabric.

2 Slipstitch, using matching thread. I rarely find an exact match in my thread collection, so use a "blending match" more often than not. Use 100 percent cotton, or a size 50 silk sewing thread. Wax the thread with beeswax to deter tangles.

3 Embroider any details.

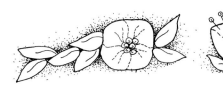

How to Slipstitch

Attach the thread to the back of the piece with several tiny stitches, then bring the needle through to the front, coming up at the edge of the appliqué.

To slipstitch, run the needle through the fold of the pressed edge of the appliqué, then pick up a thread or two of the background fabric. The stitches should be very short and nearly invisible.

Some appliqués can be sewn without pressing first. Pin or baste the appliqué to the ground fabric. Begin as above, using the tip of the needle to push the seam allowance under before making each stitch.

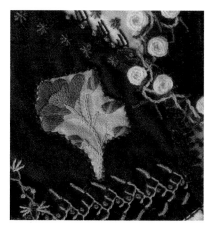

An example of broderie perse, a piece of an unfinished crewel embroidery is appliquéd onto a patch on the Horses and Roses quilt.

Other Techniques for Appliqué

1 Wool or velveteen appliqués can be finished by edging them with Buttonhole Stitch instead of turning the edges under. Do not add a seam allowance when cutting out the pieces.

2 To pad an appliqué, add a tiny pinch of stuffing when the slipstitching is nearly finished.

3 Broderie Perse is cutting out a design from a printed fabric and appliquéing it onto a different background. Use Buttonhole stitches, or turn the edges under and slipstitch around.

4 Use interesting materials for different effects. Lightweight leather, and lame fabrics are two examples. To appliqué lame, first iron a lightweight cotton fusible interfacing to the back of it.

5 To use freezer paper, cut out the appliqué design without adding seam allowances. Iron it onto the wrong side of the appliqué fabric. Cut out the fabric adding 1/8" to 1/4" seam allowance all around. Press the seam allowance to the back, over the freezer paper. Pin the appliqué to the background fabric and slipstitch around. Pull out the paper just before the stitching is finished, or cut a slit in the background fabric to remove the paper (without cutting into the appliqué), then stitch the opening closed.

6 Bias strips can be formed into elaborate Celtic knot designs, basket shapes, or used as stems or trimmings across patches. Use a bias tape maker if you need a large quantity. Pin the bias to the patch, pinning curves. Slipstitch along the edges.

A Victorian Embroidery Design

This design is an adaptation of Victorian embroidery designs with their curving stems, twining vines, and naturalistically posed flowers. Four flowers are appliquéd onto patch fabric, then embroidered details are added.

A Victorian Floral to appliqué and embroider.

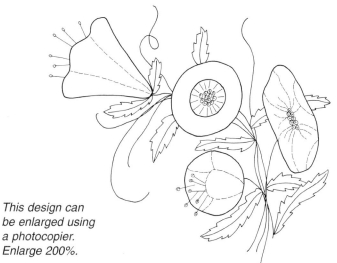

This design can be enlarged using a photocopier. Enlarge 200%.

Monogramming

NEEDED:

embroidery floss and needle, hoop, scissors.

Used to decorate household linens, Monogramming is one of the many needlearts practiced by Victorian stitchers. A finely made monogram can be an attractive enhancement on a crazy patch.

A variety of stitches can be used to embroider a monogram, the most common of them Satin, Backstitch, and Outline stitch. They are sometimes entwined with florals in Outline, Straight, Lazy Daisy, French Knot, and other stitches. Please refer to the chapter, Victorian Stitches for instructions for the individual stitches.

Use cotton, rayon, or silk floss. Very fine stitching can be done using one strand. For greater coverage, use two or three strands. Traditionally a white-on-white technique, monograms can be worked in any color or color scheme.

How to Monogram:

❶ Choose an alphabet style that is appropriate for embroidery. Two are given here, and you can also use your own handwriting.

❷ If two or more letters will be overlapped onto each other, consider making them two different sizes. Redraw the letter in the size desired. Trace each letter to be used onto tracing paper and cut them out. Taping them onto a sheet of plain paper, arrange the letters so they over-

A monogram and tea rose were combined in this shadowbox detail.

lap onto each other. Be sure the slant and spacing between them is the same, and place a ruler under them to be sure they line up. Make a final tracing.

❸ Transfer the letters to the fabric using any transfer method that will be completely concealed by embroidery stitches. The Tissue Paper Transfer Method is recommended since it will leave no marks on the fabric.

❹ Choose an embroidery option from the list below.

Techniques for Monogramming:

❶ Outline the letter in Outline stitch, and fill in solid areas with Satin or Padded Satin stitch. Victorian instructions call for making Padded Satin stitches thicker at the center of the area, and thinner at the outer edges. This is done by making more of the filler stitches towards the center, and fewer at the edges.

❷ Outline a solid letter in Backstitch and work Satin Stitch to fill in the letter, having it cover the backstitching.

❸ Outline the letter in Outline stitch and fill in solid areas with French Knots.

❹ Outline the letter with Backstitch or Outline Stitch, then work Detached Buttonhole over them. Solid areas can be filled in with French Knots or Satin Stitch.

The letter "C" was appliquéd, then embroidered in this Canadian crazy quilt detail. Collection of Rocky Mountain

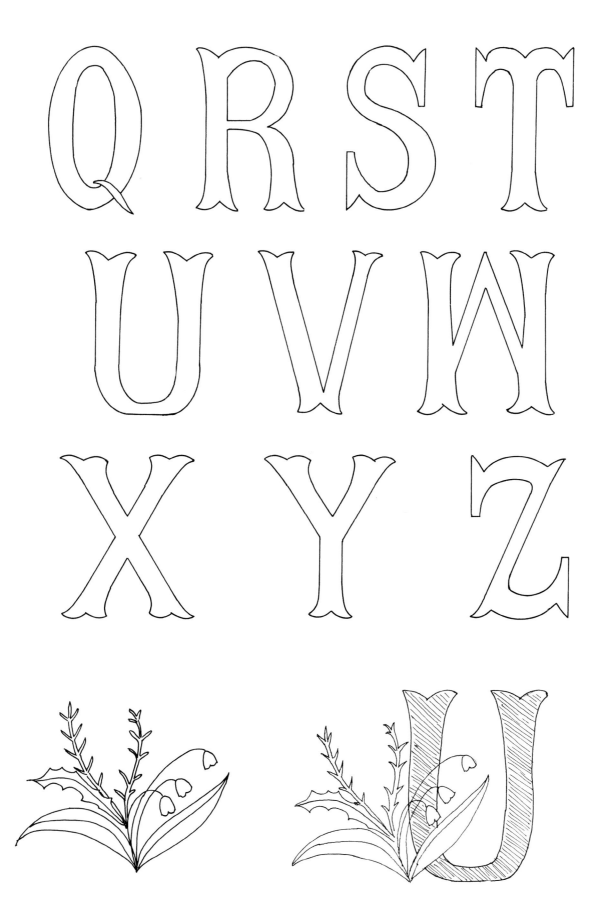

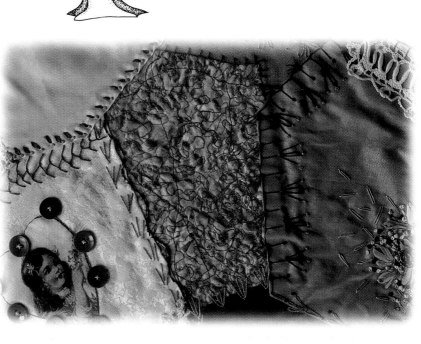

Fabrications

Texturing Fabrics

A fun and easy way to add dimensionality to a quilt top is to add folds, gathers, and scrunches to a patch as it is laid onto the foundation. I prefer to use silk fabrics for these effects. Begin with a piece of patch fabric that is too large for the space. Pin the edges of it on all but one side, leaving the fabric to bulge in the center. Choose a method below:

1 Scrunch and tack the excess fabric, creating "puffs" between tacks. To tack, use French Knots, beads, buttons, or short lines of Feather stitching.

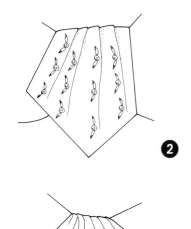

1

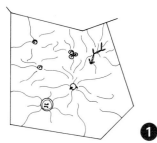

2

3

A fabricated patch was made of silk trimmings and organza fabric.

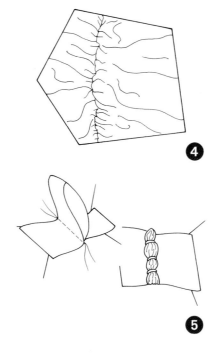

4

5

2 Arrange the free end into folds or pleats, pin and baste them in place. Later, as you embroider the quilt, silk ribbon or other embroidery can be worked on the folds to tack them in place.

3 Run a gathering thread along the free end, pull up until the end fits the space, and end off.

4 Run a gathering thread across the patch, pull up to gather, and fasten off.

5 Leaving two opposite sides of the patch free, run a basting thread as shown. Couch the excess fabric with embroidery ribbon or thread.

Finish the patch by hemming the free end, or place the adjoining patch over it. Pin, then baste.

Fabric Overlays

A sheer fabric or all-over lace can be laid onto an opaque fabric and the two used as one crazy patch. Use netting, tulle, gauzes, organza, and other sheer fabrics and laces. These are useful in landscape pieces to create the effects of fog, water, and mist. Wide laces can also be used to partly cover a patch.

A scrunched patch is held in place by embroidery.

Covering Buttons

NEEDED:
plain plastic 2 or 4 hole buttons, small pieces of fabric and cotton batting, sewing thread.

Cut the organza into two patch-size pieces, each the same. Place the silk trimmings between them (like a sandwich), and work stitching over the entire piece. Have the stitching close enough together so it adequately holds the trimmings in place.

Use the patch as you would any crazy patch, concealing its outer edges under adjoining patches.

These are not the same as the covered buttons used for clothing! These are a great way to use small leftover pieces of your hand-dyed silks. Covered buttons are attractive placed at the corners of patches, on fans, and as flower centers.

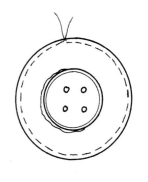

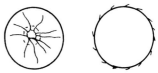

Creating Fabric with Silk Trimmings

The patch shown on the previous page was embroidered on a sewing machine set up for darning, but hand-quilting could also be used. I save all trimmings from silks, considering this material too precious to throw away! Trimmings can also be saved to stuff cloth dolls.

Covered buttons and silk tassels await placement on the Ladies and Fans quilt.

1 Cut a piece of fabric twice as large as the button. (If the button is 1 inch in diameter, cut the fabric into a 2-inch round). Cut a piece of batting the same size as the button. Run a basting thread around the outer edge of the fabric.

2 Place the batting inside the fabric and the button on top of it, and pull up the gathers. Fasten with a few small stitches, then slipstitch the button to a patch.

You can also sew on beads, or work a small motif in silk ribbon embroidery onto the fabric before it is sewn over the button.

Beads and other "hard" trims were not typically added to Victorian crazy quilts. The majority of the antique quilts feature embroidery as the sole embellishment. Beads and other trinkets are added to many modern crazy quilts and wall hangings as embellishment and to represent themes and other ideas.

Beading

Glass beads were used in great quantity by Victorian needleworkers. They used them in needlepoint, crochet, knitting, and sewed them to cross stitch pieces and into elaborate patterns on velveteen.

Wonderful highlights on crazy quilts, beads can be sewn into patterns, used as flower centers, or just scattered about. They can be added to embroidery along patch edges in place of French Knots. Use them to highlight silk ribbon and wool embroideries, and to tack ribbons and lace motifs

NEEDED:

fine needle or beading needle, beading thread, scissors, embroidery hoop, beads.

The layers of the silk jacket were quilted by sewing beads to the patch seam embroidery.

onto patches. The silk cocoon jacket was beaded to quilt the jacket layers together, a functional use for them.

Czechoslovakian glass seed beads are the most common of the many bead types available. They can be found in transparent, opaque, and silver-lined types in a range of sizes. I prefer size 11 seed beads, which almost perfectly fit a 16-count canvas for beaded needlepoint, and seem about the right size for other applications.

Add beads after embroidery is finished, otherwise threads can catch on them. Also, remember that adding quantities of glass beads to a project will add weight to it.

How to Sew on Beads

Beads added to Outline stitch highlight a feather motif on the Victorian quilt.

Beads can be sewn on one at a time, or several at once. You can also string a length of them and couch them down. Use a fine needle for tiny seed beads, and twisted nylon thread made especially for beadwork.

A supported embroidery hoop can speed the process by allowing the free use of both hands. Place the project into the hoop, and spill out a few beads onto it. To use the beads, pick them up with the needle taking care not to snag the fabrics.

Beaded Needlepoint

Beaded needlepoint takes the form of pansies, nestled into leaves of silk ribbon embroidery on the Victorian quilt.

Beaded needlepoint was a popular Victorian needleart. Worked in glass seed beads in small designs, this technique can make charming, small patch embellishments. Larger pieces can add too much weight to a quilt.

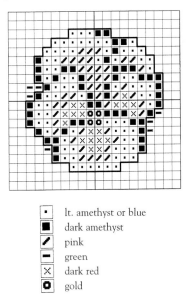

·	lt. amethyst or blue
■	dark amethyst
╱	pink
▬	green
✕	dark red
◉	gold

Work beaded pieces on a "soft" canvas such as cotton interlock. There are three ways that beads can be used in a counted design; working the entire design in beads, using beads for all except the background, and using them only for some highlights in a design.

Graphed patterns for cross stitch and needlepoint can be used.

Match the size of the bead to the canvas. For instance, size 11 seed beads fit a 16 count canvas. Using nylon beading thread, sew on the beads using a 1/2 cross stitch to have all the beads slant in the same direction.

A chart for the pansy is included here.

Charms

Charms can be added to silk ribbon and other embroideries on crazy quilts. Although they make attractive accents on wall quilts and projects such as Christmas stockings it is not advisable to use them on bedding quilts and clothing, where they are apt to catch on threads.

Buttons

Buttons of all types and sizes can be sewn onto crazy quilts, especially wall quilts and other projects.

Sew them on in clusters, overlapping them slightly. Use doll-sized mother of pearl buttons for small,

delicate touches, using them for flower and bow centers, and to tack down lace motifs and other trims.

In addition to the common plastic ones found in most sewing departments, buttons are also made of wood, bone, leather, shells, glass, metal, porcelain, and other materials. Some companies make replicas of antique buttons by using the old molds.

In the Cousins quilt, buttons are used in fastening together the layers of the quilt.

Shisha Mirrors

Shisha mirrors are sewn on by making a series of straight stitches overlapping the edges of the mirror. These are then covered with Detached Buttonhole, and additional, decorative stitches may be added around the mirrors.

Like charms, the mirrors are best placed on wall hangings and smaller projects. Handle them carefully, they are made of glass and the edges are not ground smooth.

Tassels

Tassels are fun to add to crazy quilts to decorate patches, fans, or the outer edges or corners of a quilt. They are easy to make and a great way to use up extra threads from earlier projects. A variety of threads and thread types can be combined. Try mixing shiny rayons, metallics, and matte cottons in one tassel. Or use bunka, a knitted rayon cord for tassel-making.

NEEDED:
threads, cardboard, scissors, needle.

How to Make a Tassel

Cut a piece of cardboard to the length of tassel you are making. Wrap the cardboard with thread until it is as thick as you want it to be.

Thread a needle with about one yard of the same or matching thread. Slide the needle under the wrappings, and tie a knot about 6 inches from the end of the thread at the top of the tassel.

Cut across the bottom to remove it from the cardboard.

Holding the tassel together, wrap the long end of the thread near the top. Run the needle through the tassel several times to secure, then under the wrappings through to the top. Tie the ends at the top, and make a loop for hanging.

Poking around in antiques shops can turn up some interesting trinkets to add to crazy quilt projects. Clothing and other textiles in worn condition can sometimes be salvaged for their still-good parts. (Pieces that are still good and whole should not be cut up) Some dealers sell laces and trims that have been removed from clothing and linens. Hats, belts, and gloves and fabric purses may also have parts worth using, and many types of doilies are commonly found.

Antiques awaiting a crazy quilt project: buttons, cigarette silks and felts, hankie, doily, crocheted laces.

Cigarette Silks

Cigarette silks were used as premiums in cigarette packages. In the early 1900s, cigarette advertising became highly competitive, and although it was not quite acceptable for women to smoke they played a large role in sales of cigarettes. You can probably imagine a woman fond of needlework egging her husband to buy a pack of ciggies so she could have the silk! The manufacturers of cigarettes went so far as to print suggestions for needlework projects including table covers, doilies, portiers, and clothing accessories.

There were several types of "silks" made. The smaller ones shown here were referred to by one manufacturer as "satin wonders." Close examination of these reveals a heavy base thread that is probably cotton beneath a silk satin surface. In other words, cotton-backed silk satin. The satin surface was printed by a process called chromolithography, capable of hairline details in depicting women, flags, birds, butterflies, flowers, and other subjects.

Another premium is the "felt," actually a piece of cotton flannel fabric printed with an image. Many of these were flags, but butterflies can occasionally be found. These larger pieces were not in the packages. They had to be sent for.

Although the cigarette silks and felts are part of crazy quilting jargon these days, they weren't made until the early 1900's, as the fad for crazy quilting was ending. They appear in some post-Victorian crazy quilts, and in modern ones.

The silks and felts are now quite delicate and should be handled carefully. Do not turn their edges under. To fasten them onto quilts, lay ribbons over their edges and lightly embroider along them, or tack the ribbons on with sewing thread. Fasten them on in the final stages of making the quilt, and do not sew them onto quilts that will receive active use.

Laces

Laces of many types can be found in many antiques shops, with some shops specializing in them. If you are going to cut them up, find pieces that are beyond repair, in which sections are still useable.

Also consider making your

own motifs of crochet, knitting or tatting, or bobbin or tape lace. Patterns and instructions can be found for all of these.

Hankies

Silk hankies were carried by Victorian ladies. A pretty, whole one in good condition can be tacked onto a central patch on a crazy quilt. Pieces of salvaged ones can be tucked under patches. A shadowbox is an excellent way to display antiques without having to cut and sew them.

Buttons

Antique buttons can sometimes be found in jarfuls, reasonably priced, and this is the way to buy them. You will doubtless find a place for each one on your projects! They may need washing before using. Some may be covered in tiny bits of antique fabrics–these make nice flower centers. Sew on a large one, and attach a tassel.

Needlework

Old needlework in good condition, such as crewel, needlepoint, and other types, can often be used as patches. Full-size pieces can often be used as quilt centers. Unfinished pieces that are not likely to ever be finished, can be cut up and appliquéd or used as patches. If the design seems hopelessly outdated, try adding ribbonwork, or silk ribbon embroidery to them.

Small areas of intricate detail draw the eye of the viewer. Detail of the Ladies and Fans quilt.

Creating Moments

Bringing out the fullest potential of an area of a crazy quilt - staying within that area until it is complete in itself, is what I call "creating a moment."

Much of the beauty of a fancy crazy quilt is in its details, those places on the quilt that attract the eye of the viewer.

One way to begin one of these is to place an embroidery hoop onto a selected area of the quilt. Appliqué on a photo on fabric, a cluster of ribbonwork flowers, or lace motif. Add to it using couched ribbons, silk ribbon or other embroidery, then adding some beads or buttons. Continue to add until the area seems complete, a mini work of art.

These "moments" can be very entrancing to do!

Remember to be kind to yourself.

When doing needlework, I often find myself getting so involved that I forget to notice aching bones. We're now finding that aches can turn into permanent injuries. It is important to change position often; stand up and stretch as much as necessary. Have some lively music playing, and even sit on the floor occasionally. If your neck or wrists are getting strained, find a position that causes no strain. Use adequate lighting to avoid eyestrain. Stitch in natural daylight if possible, either outdoors or by a window.

Oops, an ouch can be too late!
Bigger damage spells the fate.
Joints and bones and sight are dear.
Be kind in work to save a tear!

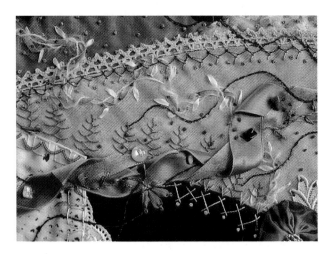

A mix of textures and materials are shown in this detail of the Landscape hanging.

Part 2:
Paint, Dye, & Transfer Methods

The Dye Experiments yield a range of colorful silks. Almost the entire bunch of silks shown here were used in the silk Ladies and Fans Quilt.

This chapter includes techniques that are the basis of textile design. Becoming a part of the fabric itself, they can be used to transform an ordinary or plain fabric into something extraordinary.

Dyeing and painting fabrics is truly an experience, and small amounts of fabric, ribbons, and trims can be done at a time. This is sometimes the only way to get the color effects you'd like to have, and achieving almost infinite ranges and shades is easy to do. An hour or two of experimentation can yield sufficient patches, ribbons, threads, and trims to make a small quilt. And do not throw away pieces that might be considered imperfect. Some of my silk dye "mistakes" became surprisingly attractive gathered flowers and yo-yos!

Following are some basic techniques that can be done with minimal tool and materials requirements.

Dyeing Silk Patches, Trims, and Ribbons

If you are looking around for some interesting and even unusual colors for patches, trims, and threads, and feeling limited by those commercially available, then definitely you must try dyeing your own silks. By doing the dye experiments that follow, you can generate shades and mixes of colors that are compatible with each other because they will share characteristics.

There are different types of dyes. One is an instant setting dye that "strikes" almost immediately. Another requires a dye-setting additive after allowing the fabrics to set for 24 hours. Both of these are easy to use, and can be done in small amounts for patch-size pieces of fabric. The instructions given below are for the instant-setting dyes. You can also use any other type of silk dye following any additional instructions that came with them.

Do each of the four dye experiments, and you will end up with 40 or more differently colored patches, enough to make a small wall quilt, several

---

MATERIALS

Instant-setting silk dyes, 1/2-oz. bottle each of red, yellow, blue, and black.
4 quarter-yard pieces of white or natural silk fabrics such as habotai, satin, jacquard, crepe.
Any desired silk ribbons, trims, threads.
1/2 cup measure.

4 small containers per experiment, jars or plastic, do not re-use in the kitchen.
Distilled water.
8 or more eye droppers.
Rubber gloves or tongs.
Large piece of plastic or plastic tablecloth to protect your work surface.

Procedure:

❶ Cover your work area with plastic. Cut each fat quarter into 12 pieces. Because they will be crazy patches they can be cut into unequal sizes. Prewash silk fabrics, threads, ribbons and trims that will be dyed, and keep them wet or damp.

❷ Follow instructions for each dye experiment following. Each experiment should yield 10 dyed silk patches. Use one eye dropper for each dye bottle, and one for each container of dye. The eye droppers are also used to stir the silks while dyeing.

❸ To dye evenly, stir the silks continuously while in the dye bath. For a mottled effect, crumple the silks into the dye, and

leave them for a couple of minutes. Then, turn them over, and leave them for a few minutes again. With either method, leave the pieces in the dye for several minutes.

❹ Remove silks from the dye with tongs, or just pick them up if you are wearing rubber gloves. Allow them to drip for a minute, then set them aside.

When finished, wash the silks with mild soap and rinse under running water. Roll them in a clean towel to remove excess moisture. Hang over a towel bar and allow to dry, then press. If you are using other than instant-setting dyes, follow instructions that came with the dyes for finishing.

❺ Clean containers, gloves, tongs, and eye droppers with soapy water, and rinse well.

Dye Experiments

With these experiments you will learn how to achieve any color or range of colors that you wish. To replicate a color, keep notes on the quantities of dye and water that were used. The second column in each experiment will result in a pastel shade of the color in the first column, and the browns in the third column will also be pastel. To create deeper browns, repeat the experiments, skipping the second column.

		Column 1	Column 2	Column 3
		To create mixed colors, add several drops of the following, and dye a piece of silk in each:	Then add the following to obtain a lighter shade of the color in column 1, and dye another piece of silk in each:	Then add a drop or two of the following to obtain browned shades, and dye another piece of silk in each:

Dye Experiment: YELLOW

Measure 1/2 cup of distilled water into a container, and add drops of yellow dye. Add and stir until the mixture is a medium yellow. Dye one piece of silk to check that this is a medium shade.

Divide the mixture into each of three containers.

	Column 1	Column 2	Column 3
Container 1	Red (= orange)	water	Blue
Container 2	Blue (= green)	water	Black & Red
Container 3	Black (= chartreuse)	water	Black

Dye Experiment: BLUE

Measure 1/2 cup of distilled water into a container, and add drops of blue dye. Add and stir until the mixture is a medium blue. Dye one piece of silk to check that this is a medium shade.

Divide the mixture into each of three containers.

	Column 1	Column 2	Column 3
Container 1	Red (= royal purple)	water	Black & Yellow
Container 2	Yellow (= green)	water	Red (= lt. moss green)
Container 3	Black (= deep blue)	water	Black

Dye Experiment: RED

Measure 1/2 cup of distilled water into a container, and add drops of red dye. Add and stir until the mixture is a medium red. Dye one piece of silk to check that this is a medium shade.

Divide the mixture into each of three containers.

	Column 1	Column 2	Column 3
Container 1	Yellow (= orange)	water	Blue
Container 2	Blue (= purple)	water	Black
Container 3	Black	water	Black

Dye Experiment: BLACK

Measure 1/2 cup of distilled water into a container, and add drops of black dye. Add and stir until the mixture is a medium gray. Dye one piece of silk to check that this is a medium shade.

Divide the mixture into each of three containers.

	Column 1	Column 2	Column 3
Container 1	Red	water	Blue
Container 2	Blue, Yellow and 1 or 2 drops of Red	water	Black
Container 3	Yellow and 1 drop of Red	water	Red

Tips and Ideas for Dyeing

❶ Spread out some silk ribbons and trims on your plastic-covered work surface. Have a spray bottle handy to keep them dampened. As you do the dye experiments, place drops of dye randomly and spaced apart on the ribbons and trims. Select colors to obtain multi-hued ribbons and trims.

❷ Some of the Dye Experiment colors will overlap, for instance, green will be derived from both the yellow and the blue experiments, but you can make them different shades each time by adjusting amounts.

❸ You may find that the black experiments yield the most interesting shades including teal, mauve, dusty green and purple. You may want to experiment further to find other shades.

❹ Working inside a cardboard box, draw a popsicle stick across a dye-loaded toothbrush, splattering dye on a piece of silk.

❺ Tie strings or fasten pieces of silk with paper clips before placing them into the dye to achieve tie-dye effects.

❻ Lay a large, wet piece of fabric on your plastic-covered work surface. Drip onto it dye mixtures or dye straight from the bottle, allowing the colors to

Using dye to create unusual patch fabrics and ribbons.

run into each other. Leave the fabric in place until the dyes set.

❼ Add water to a dye bath, adding several times and dyeing with each addition in order to get lighter shades of that color. Especially do this if you've found a color you really like.

❽ Overdye already colored silks—either pieces you've done, or commercially dyed silks.

❾ Lay a patch-size piece of dampened fabric onto your work surface. Sprinkle salt on the fabric, then, using an eye dropper, place drops of a dye mixture onto it. Allow the dye to set for several minutes, then rinse thoroughly.

Painting

Painting was a skill cultivated by Victorian ladies who did some of their paintings on silk or velvet fabric, and included them in crazy quilts. Sometimes the border of a crazy quilt was beautifully painted.

The Victorians used oil paints. The acrylic paints we have now are more practical, easier and less messy to use. Acrylics are water-based, meaning they can be thinned and cleaned up with water. However, unlike other water based paints such as watercolors and tempera, after

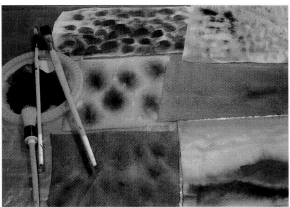

Applying paint to fabric can yield some interesting results.

acrylics dry on the fabric they are not likely to wash out, especially if they are heat-set.

Purchase acrylic paints in artist's tubes, or in small containers that are sold for stenciling. Red, yellow, blue, black, and white make a complete set from which any color can be mixed. See the section on color theory in the chapter, Natural Elegance for how to achieve different colors by mixing the primary and secondary colors.

It isn't necessary to be able to paint scenes,

On a mid-1800's crazy quilt, a rose was painted on black velvet. Detail. The Brick Store Museum, Kennebunk, Maine.

Two miniature paintings by Kim Kovaly of The Willow shop, Limerick, Maine, are beautiful additions to a crazy quilt, but require skill with paints and brushes. The Willow Shop.

A painting on velvet makes an elaborate sashing in this mid-1800's crazy quilt. Detail. The Brick Store Museum, Kennebunk, Maine.

flowers, and other objects. Painting can be used to enhance patch fabrics and create backgrounds for embroidery and other embellishment. You can paint lines and brush strokes that swoop, curve, overlap, fade in and out, and many other fantastical effects that are easy to do. These can make excellent backgrounds for embroidery of all types, landscape quilts, and just interesting patches.

Paints can be used on many fabric types such as cotton, rayon, silk, wool, and others. Begin with scrap fabrics to try some of the following techniques. Remember that embroidery and other embellishments can be added later to enhance your efforts. You can also cut up the pieces and use them in sections.

Heat-setting acrylic paint

Acrylic paints must be heat-set to make them permanent. Before heat-setting, allow the paint to air dry at least 24 hours. Place a press cloth over the painted area. Heat the iron to the correct temperature setting for the fabric, and hold the iron on for 30 seconds. Repeat to cover all of the painted area. The fabric should be left again for 24 hours before it is washed.

Follow the instructions that are on the paint container for clean up. Acrylic paints are water soluble, but are permanent after they dry. For this reason, brushes and work surfaces should be cleaned with soap and water before the paint dries.

MATERIALS

Acrylic paints in tubes or jars in red, blue, yellow, black and white.
Artist's brushes in a variety of sizes.

Bowls or small pots for mixing.
Water.
Pallette or plate for blending colors.

Prewash the fabric, allow it to dry, and press.

There are two basic techniques for painting: wet brush, and dry brush. For dry brush painting, slightly dampen the brush, then dip it into the paint and brush the paint onto the fabric. Depending on how much paint is on the brush, this will leave broad or wispy brush strokes on the fabric. This technique can be used on dry or dampened fabric. If you brush the paint onto very wet fabric, it will act like a wash, and spread.

For the wet brush technique, dip the brush into water and leave it very wet. Use paint that is thinned with water. As the paint is brushed onto the fabric, it will spread out as the fabric absorbs the moisture and the paint runs. This is called a "wash," and achieves a similar effect to dyeing the fabric. Different effects can be obtained by having the fabric either damp, or very wet.

Try the following wet and dry brush experiments using the colors of your choice:

1 Using the dry brush technique, randomly brush paint onto fabric that is dry or slightly damp. Allow it to dry completely. Now, go back over it with a wash.

2 The reverse of 1, paint a wash onto wet fabric, and allow it to dry thoroughly. Then, dry brush in any pattern over the wash.

3 In separate areas of the pallette, mix two different wash colors. Dampen the fabric, or have it wet. Brush on the washes side by side and allow them to run into each other.

4 While the paint is still wet, lift the fabric to allow the paint to run. This can be done with any wash. The wetter the fabric, the more the paint will run. Leave the fabric to dry.

Painting techniques:

1 Stroking with the brush, or dabbing with it will achieve different results, especially using the dry brush technique.

2 Placing two or more colors on the same brush without mixing them together can be used for rainbow-like effects.

3 Instead of brushes, use your fingers, foam brushes, or other implements to apply the paint.

4 Use sponges, crumpled paper, or other materials to dab the paint onto the fabric.

5 Drip paint onto the fabric.

Stencilling

Applying paint to velveteen fabric using stencils produces a clean-edge design with an almost luminescent effect from the paint. I like this effect, but you can also simply paint on the velveteen without using stencils. The stencil designs here are finished with embroidery.

I use freezer paper to make stencils. It is inexpensive, readily available, easy to cut, and the plastic side of the paper prevents the paint from wearing through. Although it will not hold up to heavy use, it is fine for one or two uses. If you are going to use a stencil for more than this, cut it from a sturdier material. To reuse a stencil, first allow it to dry completely.

The type of velveteen I prefer to use is a low-napped all-cotton type, rather than the high plush types.

Tools and materials for stenciling on fabrics. A piece of velvet ribbon was painted along its edges.

MATERIALS
Velveteen fabric, prewashed.
Freezer paper, pencil.
Smooth corrugated cardboard larger than the design.
Stencil brush about 3/4" to 1" in diameter.
Acrylic paints in red, blue, yellow, black and white.
Pallette or substitute.
Sewing pins.
Craft knife and smooth cardboard.
Water.

Instructions:

1 Lay a piece of freezer paper over the design to be used, and draw the outlines that will be cut out. Place this on the smooth cardboard or other cutting surface, and cut along the lines using the craft knife. (The freezer paper can be ironed onto smooth fabrics. Do not iron it onto velveteen or other napped fabrics, it will pull out the pile when the paper is removed).

2 Place the velveteen onto the corrugated cardboard, then the stencil on top with the plastic side down. Pin into the cardboard to hold everything in place.

3 Mix the color to be used. For leaves, mix yellow and blue to get green. The green can be shaded with a drop of black, or tinted with white. A drop of red can be added to get a warm, mossy green. Add extra blue if you prefer a teal, or blue-green.

It is advisable to add plenty of white to colors that will be stenciled onto dark velveteens so they show up well. Mixed colors can be left partly unmixed, to give a varied effect to the painting. Do not add much water to the paint. If it is too wet, the color will bleed under the stencil.

4 Dab the brush in the paint, and again alongside the paint on the pallette to remove excess. The brush should be dry, and there should not be a lot of paint on it. Holding the brush vertically, stencil the design by tapping the brush repeatedly until sufficient color is transferred. Remove the stencil and allow the paint to dry.

To do the Hollyhock design, first place pinholes through both patterns at the dots. Place pins through these dots into the cardboard for the leaves stencil. Keep the pins in place when the stencil is removed. Allow the leaves to dry. Place the flower stencil over the leaves, placing the stencil onto the pins at the dots. Mix a rosy or peachy color and stencil the flowers.

Allow the stenciled design to dry, heat-set, and embroider the details.

Work stem in outline stitch

Transfer dots and use to align flowers with leaves

Rubbings

This technique was used for the Butterstamp quilt. I got the idea at The Butterstamp Shop in Wiscasset, Maine where I found plaques, curtain tie-backs, and other objects made from butterstamp impressions. At the same shop were supplies for gravestone rubbings. And I thought, what a great way to transfer the beautifully carved butterstamp designs onto fabric!

A butterstamp wrapped in plastic for doing rubbings on silk fabrics. Dye pastels are from Pentel. Butterstamps collection of Paul Baresel.

MATERIALS

Fabric crayons or pastels (containing dye).
Objects with 3D surfaces: wood buttermolds, gravestones, leaves, lace, etc.
Lightweight plastic if the surface must be protected from the dye.
Iron, and plain paper

Instructions:

Do not use plain crayons or pastels for this. The crayons or pastels must have dye in them to be permanent on fabric.

Follow any instructions with the crayons or pastels.

If you are using wooden butterprints, first cover them with a thin plastic to avoid dyeing the wood. To do a rubbing, hold a piece of silk fabric over the print. Hold tightly, and if necessary, secure the fabric with a rubber band to prevent shifting. Lightly rub the crayon or pastel over the fabric until the design shows up.

Remove the fabric from the print, and iron it between two sheets of clean, white paper on an ironing board that is adequately protected. (Protect your ironing board with extra paper or fabric). This sets the dye and removes the grease from the crayon. Repeat, using clean paper to be sure the grease is removed.

Wash the pieces separately, dry and press.

Patches on the Butterstamp quilt are rubbings taken from antique butterstamps.

Photographic images on fabric is not a new idea. Crazy quilts of the late 1800's often include an image or two that is a photo on silk.

Now, a similar effect can be had by using a special transfer paper. An image is photocopied onto it, then ironed onto fabric. Silk ribbon and other embroidery can be worked around the image on fabric. Add trims, charms, beads, and buttons to embellish.

MATERIALS

Photo transfer paper.
Color photocopier.
Image: color photo or antique postcard.
Iron.

Instructions:

Follow the instructions with the transfer paper. Basically, you will take the paper and your images to a business that does color photocopying, and have them copied onto the transfer paper. You then take this home, and iron the image onto fabric. Each image is good only once, so position carefully, making sure the fabric is not out of kilter.

If you are placing the image onto silk fabric, try a piece of scrap fabric with the iron setting for the time indicated. If the silk scorches, place a sheet of plain paper between fabric and iron. If your test comes out OK, do the transfer.

You may find that some color photos transferred to a quilt appear very bright, and sometimes even garish. To tone down a "loud" photo, trim away some background, border it with embroidery, or paint around with a soft wash to blend it in. If the photos are transferred onto pastel-color fabric, the color of the fabric will show through the light areas of the photo.

Photos of roses from my garden, and antique postcards are waiting to be photocopied onto transfer paper. A rose photo transferred onto the Ladies and Fans quilt has silk ribbon embroidered leaves added to it.

Text and Crazy Quilts

Giving people something to read on a crazy quilt seems to draw them to it. They simply have to read the words! Text can be applied in a number of ways including pens and crayons containing dye, and with outline and other embroidery stitches. If you are using pens, some fabrics are easier to write on than others. For the best results, a smooth cotton should be used. Always heat-set any paint or dye materials that are added to fabric, including fabric pens. To embroider the letters, write the words to be used on a sheet of plain paper, then use the tissue paper transfer method to place them onto the fabric.

You can use:

names of people and pets
poetry
quotes
place names such as states, cities, countries
words relevant to the theme of a quilt

Documenting a quilt.

Documentation is important if a quilt survives through many years. Many antique quilts that have been abandoned, donated, or sold out of the original family are not signed or dated. It is impossible to document where and how they originated, and because of this it is a difficult task for historians to study the place of quilts and quiltmaking in our history.

Your initials, the year the quilt is finished, and the city or state the quilt is made in are important bits of information that can be embroidered or painted on the patches of the quilt. Additional documentation can be written on a piece of fabric such as muslin, using fabric pens. Neatly hem the fabric and slipstitch it to the quilt's backing.

A method that was used for documenting fundraiser quilts was to sew a small pocket to the backing of the quilt for inserting notes written on paper.

Wording placed on a quilt can indicate names, places, and objects.

Finishing Touches

The variety of ways antique crazy quilts are assembled is yet another demonstration that this type of quilt was a creative phenomenon. Made with or without battings, the Victorian crazy quilted tops were finished with borders, bindings, laces, ruffles, or other edgings. They were tied with embroidery or sewn stitches, pearl threads, ribbons, and sometimes were not tied at all. There was no preconceived manner of finishing a crazy quilt.

Because several methods for each step of the finishing are given, please read through the chapter before beginning so you can choose an appropriate procedure for your quilt.

Adding a Border

Borders on some of the antique crazy quilts were extravagantly done, with corner fans, paintings on velvet, embroidery, ribbonwork, patchwork, appliqué, and other techniques. Even plain velvet borders have much to offer these quilts, the plush of the velvet adding a softening touch. Borders act as a frame, provide additional

The 1898 quilt shown here is one of many crazy quilts bordered and backed with cotton sateen fabric. This quilt has a batting. Collection of the author.

area to embellish, expand the size of the quilt, and in some cases, support its theme.

Themes portrayed on a quilt can be reflected by a border design. Early America is the theme suggested by the border of the Butterstamp quilt, with its folk-style patchwork. A trailing vine of roses surrounds the Horses and Roses quilt, and a feminine ruffle decks out the Ladies and Fans quilt.

Borders are sewn onto the quilt after patch embellishment and embroidery are finished.

Straight stitch fans decorate the velvet border of the 1862 "White Rose" crazy quilt. Detail. Photographed at Shiretown Antique Center, Alfred, Maine.

Planning the Border

Most of my borders are planned while the quilt is in progress. Beginning with a rough idea of the finished size of the quilt, I try to visualize how different types of borders will look, sketching out some of these ideas. Eventually a particular idea strikes me as something I'd really like to try. Working up a small section as a sample is usually enough to indicate whether the idea will work or not.

If the quilt is for a bed, the dimensions of the border may already have been decided. For other types of quilts, this decision can be reserved for last, when the top is nearing completion. At this point, border colors and widths can be "tried on" the quilt, to determine what will look best.

"Trying on" Borders

To choose a border fabric, take your completed or nearly completed quilt top to a fabric store. Using a cutting table, unroll about a yard or so off a bolt, fold the cut edge under, and lay the quilt top over this leaving a border's width of the fabric protruding. Try several different fabrics and compare how they look with the quilt. Look for both a color and a width that will best enhance your quilt. Be sure to check your color choice in natural lighting before buying.

The principles of color theory given in the chapter, Natural Elegance, also apply to the border. Use black or dark colors for a border that will tend to recede, causing the quilt top to come forward visually, highlighting it. A neutral color will enlarge the quilt without significantly affect-

ing its color scheme. If the border consists of similar colors to those in the quilt top, as in the Butterstamp quilt, a narrow contrasting sashing can be added to differentiate the two.

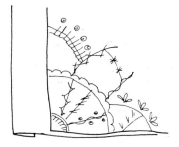

Fabrics for Borders

Cotton sateen must have been considered a "utilitarian" fabric in the late 1800s. It was used for backings and borders on many crazy quilts, and also for vest linings. Now, this gorgeous fabric seems all too rare, unfortunately hard to find. Its weight, satin surface, and elegant drape make it a perfect choice for a finishing a quilt.

Many other fabric types also make excellent borders including velvet, velveteen, satin, silks noil or dupion, linens and wools. Some drapery and decorating fabrics, including bengaline, moiré, and damask with their attractively textured and patterned surfaces are additional possibilities. Take into consideration a fabric's weight, drape, fiber content, and care features, and be sure it will be suitable for any embellishment method that will be used.

Figuring Yardage for Borders

Determine the width of the yardage you will be purchasing. Cottons and acetates are often available as 44-inch widths, but are sometimes up to 60 inches wide.

If you are making a small quilt, and the longest border piece fits across the yardage, up to 9-inch wide borders (including seam allowances) can be cut out of 1 yard of fabric.

For larger quilts, cut the border from the length of the fabric. Purchase the length of fabric required for the longest border piece.

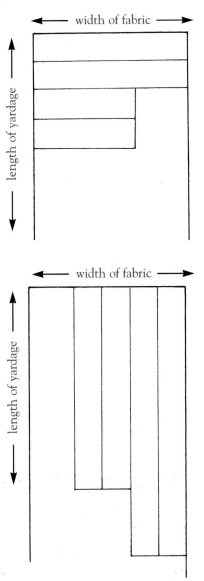

Piecing Fabric for Borders

Whenever possible, I prefer to have my borders of continuous lengths of fabric. This is may require purchasing more fabric, but I think it gives a smoother result. Any left over fabric is saved for future quilts and projects.

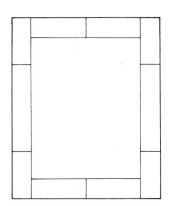

If you are going to piece the border, make the pieces match on both sides of the quilt. Divide the border length in half or in thirds being sure to add seam allowances to the ends of each section. Sew the sections together, then sew the borders to the quilt.

Backing Fabrics, Dimensions and Yardage

Many of the quilts I've made are backed with calico fabrics purchased for traditional quilting. This quilting experience begins and ends with an Amish wall hanging that is tucked away in a closet patched and mostly unquilted. Having discovered that "quilting" has creative counterparts that I enjoy much more, chances are it will stay there unless I choose to work it into a crazy quilt.

width of fabric

length of yardage

Unless you want the back of your quilt to serve a purpose, a quilt's backing can be almost any good fabric. Choose a suitable fabric if you will have signatures, documentation, a pocket, ribbon bows or other embellishment on the back of the quilt.

If you are making a knife-edge quilt, use the same fabric as the border to have it blend in, or as in the Butterstamp quilt, use a contrasting color so a sliver of it shows on the front. This hairline, if it is a dark color, will keep a light-colored wall quilt from blending into the wall.

Cotton sateen was often used in the antique crazy quilts, and is an excellent choice of backing fabric. For a quilt that will be warm and cozy, try a velveteen or corduroy backing. A wool quilt can have either a wool or cotton backing. Silk quilts that have silk batting should also have a silk backing fabric in order to help hold the batting in place.

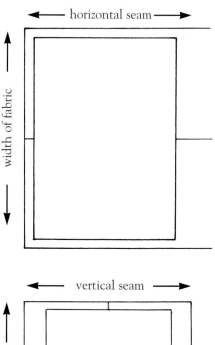

horizontal seam

width of fabric

vertical seam

length of yardage

To calculate the amount of yardage to purchase for backing, first measure the quilt. If the quilt width is the same or less than the width of the fabric, simply purchase the amount required for the length of the quilt.

If the backing must be pieced, purchase fabric that is twice the width of the quilt to have a horizontal seam or, purchase twice the length of the quilt to have a vertical seam.

Always buy a little extra in case of shrinkage.

Interfacing the Border

In order for a border to hang properly, it should be adjusted to approximate the thickness of the quilt top with its multiple layers. If the border is too floppy for a firmly made top, or too firm for a drapey one, it won't look right.

To make this adjustment, interface the border using the same type of foundation fabric that was used in the quilt. Cut the foundation the dimensions of each border piece, place them wrong sides together and proceed as if they were one fabric.

Pressing the Seams

If embroidery will be worked along seams, press them open. If embroidery will not be used, the seams that join the border to the quilt top can be pressed towards the border.

A Plain Border

This border is simple to make. Determine the width of the border including seam allowances. To purchase yardage, two borders will equal the length of the quilt top, and two will be the width of the quilt plus two border widths.

❶ Measure the length of the quilt, including seam allowances. Cut two pieces of border fabric this length. Cut two of foundation fabric and place one of these on the back of each border piece, and handle them as if they were one. Sew each side border to the quilt top. Press the seams.

❷ Measure the width of the quilt including the side borders. Cut two pieces of border

fabric this length. Cut two of foundation fabric, place one on the back of each border piece and handle as one. Sew each to top and bottom of quilt. Press the seams.

A border made with corner blocks is one of many ways that crazy quilts were finished. This one is attractively edged in gold cording. Detail of an 1885 crazy quilt. The Brick Store Museum, Kennebunk, Maine.

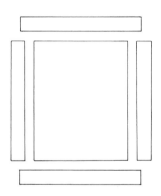

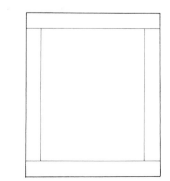

Feather and Herringbone stitches were used along block seams after they were sewn together in this antique wool crazy quilt. This quilt was finished without adding a border. Owned by Avalon Antiques, photographed at Arundel Antiques, Arundel, Maine. Photo by Paul Baresel.

A Border with Corner Blocks

Make this the same as the above method except make two borders the same length, and two the same as the width of the quilt. Sew on the side borders. Make 4 corner blocks, lining them as above with foundation fabric. Sew one corner to each end of the top and bottom pieces, then sew to the quilt top.

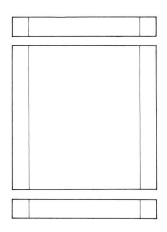

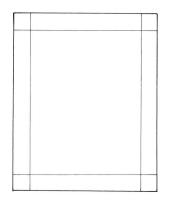

A Border with Mitered Corners

Determine the width of the border. To purchase yardage, two borders will equal the length of the quilt top and two border widths, and the other two will equal the width of the quilt plus two border widths.

1 Cut two pieces of border fabric the length of the quilt plus two border widths and seam allowances. Cut two of foundation fabric and place one of these on the back of each border piece.

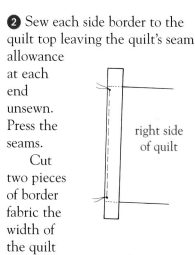

2 Sew each side border to the quilt top leaving the quilt's seam allowance at each end unsewn. Press the seams.

Cut two pieces of border fabric the width of the quilt plus two border widths and seam allowances and repeat instruction 1 to add the top and bottom borders.

right side of quilt

3 Place one corner of the quilt on the ironing board. Fold back the two adjoining borders, and make a crease exactly where the seam will be. Repeat for the remaining three corners.

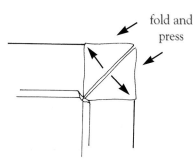

fold and press

4 Sew each corner as follows: with right sides together, line up the crease of each border section and pin. Sew from the outer edge to the inner edge. Trim away excess fabric, and press the seam open.

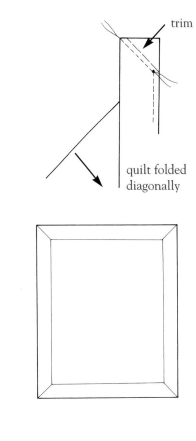

trim

quilt folded diagonally

Embroidered or Appliquéd Border

Before adding batting and backing, work any embroidery or appliqué design.

Scalloped Patchwork Border and Backing

Finish embroidery and embellishment on the quilt top, then add a narrow sashing if desired. Set the piece aside.

Choose the fabrics to be used for the patchwork border.

The pattern for the scalloped patches is 2 inches wide to fit a quilt top that is an even number of inches in width and length. Divide the length of the quilt top (minus the seam allowances) by 2 to get the number of blocks required. If the sewn row of patches doesn't exactly fit the quilt top, the first and last patches can be made either wider or narrower. Or, adjust the width of the pattern by finding a width that is evenly divisible by the quilt top dimensions.

The Butterstamp quilt is a theme quilt displaying folk art images; 1994. Collection of Paul Baresel.

Assemble the border as follows:

❶ Copy or trace the pattern onto plain paper and cut it out. Cut out the required number of patches for each border length, and cut an equal number out of foundation fabric. Place one foundation piece on the back of each patch. Sew patches together to make each border. Press seams open.

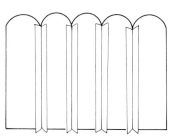

❷ Sew the side borders to the quilt top. Sew the corner blocks to the ends of the top and bottom borders, and sew to the quilt top. Press the seams. Work embroidery along the patch seams.

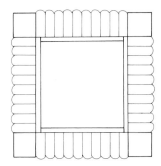

❸ The easiest way to install a backing is to make it in two pieces, as in the diagram. Be sure to allow for seam allowances to join the sections. Cut the backing slightly larger than the quilt top.

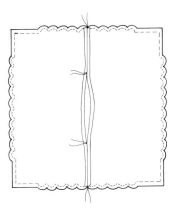

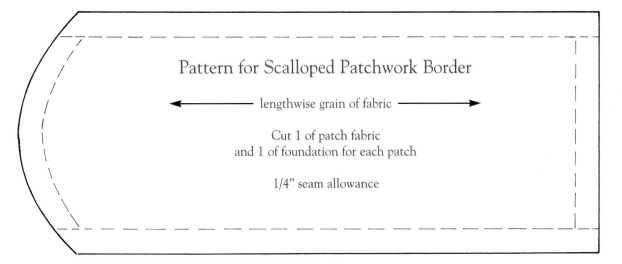

Pattern for Scalloped Patchwork Border

← lengthwise grain of fabric →

Cut 1 of patch fabric
and 1 of foundation for each patch

1/4" seam allowance

With right sides together, sew the seam of the backing leaving the center 24 inches or so open. Press the seam open. Place the backing right sides together with the quilt top, having the quilt on top. Pin carefully all around.

4 Taking your time, sew around the entire outer edge. For the best results, end stitching at each patch seam, and begin stitching on the following patch without leaving a gap.

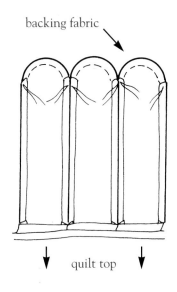

backing fabric

quilt top

5 Trim excess backing fabric, and trim seams. Turn the quilt right side out, and carefully press the scalloped edges. Slipstitch the center of the backing closed.

6 Finish the quilt by tying the quilt top, having the ties on the back. Embroidery stitches can be worked along the sashings. Here, Straight stitch fans were used.

Types of Batting.

A batting can be added along with the backing after the quilt top is finished. Battings are entirely optional; most Victorian crazies did not have them.

There are many types of batting available. My preferences are always with the natural fiber types, such as silk, wool, and cotton.

Silk battings come and go. Years ago I purchased "silk caps" that had to be carefully tugged open. As they were pulled, the fibers gradually released, creating a batting that seemed skimpy but proved to be of sufficient loft for a silk quilt. Then, there were silk battings that could be used straight out of the package. Battings are the same as carded fiber ready for spinning, called rovings. These can be pulled apart to be used as batting. Look for battings and rovings that are made of long fibers if they are to be tugged apart.

Silk crazy quilts require only a thin layer of batting that should be placed between two layers of silk fabrics. Silk batting clings to silk fabrics, helping to hold the layers in place. If, in tying the quilt, the batting comes through the fabric along with the thread, do not keep pulling or the entire batting could come out (how's that for magic!?). Instead, with a sharp embroidery scissors, trim it very closely to the quilt top, then pull up on the fabric to work the batting to the inside of the quilt.

Wool battings have more loft than cotton, and are excellent for bed coverings used in cool climates. Store these quilts in a cedar trunk if they are not in use during the summer.

Cotton battings are excellent for wall hangings, or any size quilt. They are easy to handle because they are not lofty. Some cotton battings must be prewashed to shrink them and to remove the oil from the cotton seeds.

Use only battings that allow plenty of space between ties or quilting stitches. Those that must be closely quilted are not suitable for crazy quilts.

Cotton flannel fabric may be used to add a little extra loft or warmth in place of a batting. Velveteen or corduroy can also be used for the backing fabric for extra warmth and weight.

Joining sections of batting to create a larger piece is done the same for all types. Edges are butted together, sometimes by fluffing each to blend them into each other. Never overlap two pieces of batting, as this can make a long bump in the quilt. Loosely stitching the join with long stitches - about two or more inches in length - will help to keep the pieces joined. Otherwise, be sure to use sufficient ties when tying the quilt.

To Add Lace or Ruffled Edgings

Some antique crazies are made all the more attractive by their lace and ruffled edgings. To add this type of edging to a quilt, choose a cotton or rayon venice lace, or an heirloom cotton lace. Or, better yet, crochet, Battenberg, bobbin, tat, or knit a lace edging if you have any of these skills. Choose a pattern in a width that is suitable for the quilt. Some laces such as the cotton net lace used in the Doll's Quilt are often sold flat, and must be gathered, then sewn into a seam. Start with a length of lace that is 1 1/2 times the finished length, and gather it by running a basting thread along the long raw edge. While pinning the lace to the quilt top, draw up the basting thread, gathering the lace to fit.

Use a knife-edge quilt finish to sew lace into a seam. To add an edging with a finished edge such as crochet, simply stitch it by hand to the finished edge of the quilt.

Pleat, or add extra gathers to the lace or ruffle at each corner of the quilt to have sufficient fullness to turn the corner.

Knife-edge Quilt Finish.

This method creates an edge into which laces and trims may be inserted. It can be used on a quilt top with or without borders.

1 To the finished quilt top, with right sides together, pin any lace or trim that will be sewn into the seam. Sew together the short ends, or overlap and curve the ends outward so the raw ends will be sewn into the seam allowance.

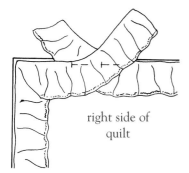

right side of
quilt

2 With right sides together, place the backing fabric on the quilt top. If a batting is added, place it on top of the backing. Pin.

3 Sew around, leaving an opening large enough to turn the quilt. Trim corners, and trim the seam allowance if necessary. Turn right sides out, press. Sew the opening closed.

Stack and Bind

Binding is a traditional method of finishing a quilt that was sometimes used to finish Victorian crazy quilts. A binding can be used in place of, or in addition to a border.

Assemble the quilt layers with wrong sides together; quilt top, (batting if used), and backing. Pin, then baste around the outer edges. Measure around the quilt to determine the required yardage.

Detail of the 1890's quilt. Courtesy of The Kirk Collection, Omaha, NE. Photo by Nancy T. Kirk.

1 Make or purchase sufficient 1/2-inch wide bias binding.
2 Open out the binding and sew it with right sides together to the sides of the quilt top, then cut it even with the top and bottom edges of the quilt. Press, folding the bias to the back of the quilt. Pin, and slipstitch invisibly.
3 Sew the bias to the top and bottom of the quilt, leaving about 1/2 inch extra at each end. Fold in the ends and slipstitch for a neat finish. Press and slipstitch as before.

This 1890's quilt was edged with a simple binding. Courtesy of The Kirk Collection, Omaha, NE. Photo by Nancy T. Kirk.

right side
of quilt

back side
of quilt

How to make Bias Binding

Making a bias tape for binding is easy to do, and many different types of fabrics can be used for this including silks, cottons, rayons, and lightweight wool.

❶ Begin with a square of fabric. A 36-inch square will yield 24 lengths from 12 inches to 1-1/3 yards long that are 1-1/2 inches wide, sufficient bias for most quilts.

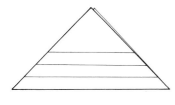

❷ Fold the fabric diagonally as shown.

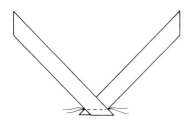

❸ Press a crease along the fold, then cut along it. Measure, and cut strips as needed. A 1/2-inch wide binding is made of 1-1/2-inch strips to have 1/4-inch seam allowances. Cut the strip slightly wider if more allowance is needed.

❹ Place the strips right sides together and sew 1/4-inch seams as shown. Press the seams open or to one side.

❺ To press, first fold the strip in half lengthwise and press the fold. Then, turn in each long raw edge 1/4 inch and press.

Self-binding

Here, the backing fabric is folded to the front of the quilt, forming a self-binding that is slipstitched.

❶ Cut the backing 1-1/2 inches larger on each side than the quilt top including borders if it has them. This will add 3 inches to the length and width dimensions of the quilt top. Place the backing and quilt with wrong sides together. If a batting is used, have that in place also. Pin.

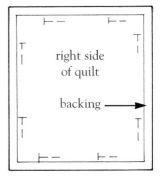

❷ Fold the backing in 1/2 an inch, and fold again onto the quilt top and pin. Fold corners neatly. Slipstitch invisibly all around.

Tying the Quilt

After assembly, the layers of the crazy quilt must be fastened together. The following methods are the same as those used on the Victorian quilts. You can choose one method or combine several.

First, lay the quilt out flat on a clean floor or other surface that supports the entire quilt. Press it lightly if necessary, and check that both sides lie absolutely smooth. If the quilt is large, safety-pin baste in a few places.

❶ With sewing thread and needle, and the quilt right side up, make small tacking stitches here and there over the entire top, having them about 4 inches or so apart. Make the stitches so they are

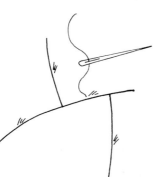

Ways to tie a crazy quilt, including adding stitches, thread and ribbon ties. Vertical strips of cotton fabric help to support a hanging quilt.

An unusual application of crazy quilting: the backing of this antique wool quilt was crazy quilted of black fabrics and embroidered in bright threads. The red stitches are quilting stitches used to join the layers. Detail. Courtesy of The Kirk collection, Omaha, NE. Photo by Nancy T. Kirk.

concealed along the edges of the patches, or under embroidery.

2 Many of the antique quilts have ties that are knotted on the back of the quilt. With the quilt wrong side up, thread a needle with a length of thread, pearl cotton, yarn, or ribbon, and make small stitches about 5-6 inches apart. Cut the thread in the middle between the stitches, and tie the ends. Use square, not granny knots so they won't come loose.

In case you don't want the threads of the ties showing on the surface of the quilt, make the ties "in the ditch," or in the seams between patches. Have the quilt right side up, bring the threaded needle up from the back to the front, and take a stitch to the back.

3 Add embroidery stitches to the face of the quilt, working them through all layers. Thread ends should be finished with a few tiny stitches (no knots) on the back.

4 If the quilt has a batting, the batting can be quilted to the backing fabric with quilting stitches (short running stitch). After quilting, place the quilt top on it with wrong sides together and sew a binding around the quilt. A few ties can then be added.

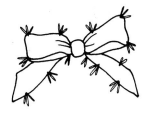

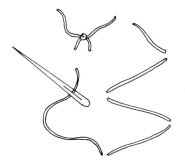

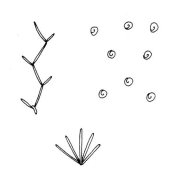

Ties, small stitches, and the ends of embroidery threads can be concealed under small bows tied of 1/4-inch to 1/2-inch wide ribbon, sewn or tacked to the quilt backing.

ABOVE: A pillow made of soft rose, peach, and blue shades will fit into almost any decorating scheme.

Pillow

BELOW: This antique block was formed into a pincushion in the shape of a pillow. Note the unusual stitches. Photographed at The Barn at Cape Neddick, Maine.

MATERIALS

Pillow form the desired size.
Muslin foundation the size of the pillow form plus seam allowances.
Backing fabric the size of the foundation plus about 6 extra inches in one direction.
Optional - edging (fringe or lace), sufficient yardage to go around the pillow.
Patch fabrics in 8 or more colors.
Size 8 pearl cotton in 8 or more colors.
Trims, laces as desired.
Velcro or snap closures.
Sewing thread.

Pillows are easy to make and are a marvelous way of displaying a singular block of crazy quilting. The following pattern can be made the size of your choice. Before beginning the pillow top, purchase a pillow form and make the pillow the same size. If you are a beginner, a small pillow of about 12 inches square is a good size to start with. The one shown here is 18 inches square. It is backed with rose-colored cotton velveteen, and a heavy cotton fringe was sewn into the seams.

Choose fabrics that are washable, and trims that will not catch on anything.
Use 1/2-inch seam allowances for assembly.
Instructions:

❶ Patch the foundation according to the method of your choice. Embellish and embroider the patched pillow top.

❷ Have the backing fabric the same width as the patched pillow top, but 6 inches longer. See the diagram. Cut the backing in half. To hem each, fold under 1/4 inches of each cut edge twice, then sew along the folds.

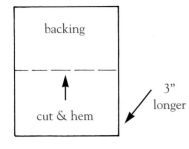

❸ With right sides together, pin lace or fringe around the pillow top, finishing the raw ends.

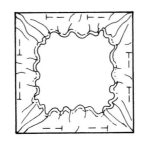

❹ With right sides together, pin the backing pieces onto the pillow top matching side, top and bottom edges. The backing will overlap in the middle of the pillow. Sew around. Turn the piece right side out, and insert the pillow form. Sew on Velcro or snap closures to the overlapped edge of the backing.

How to Hang a Wall Quilt

Smaller quilts need only a rod pocket placed along the upper edge of the back of the quilt, and a dowel placed through it. To make a rod pocket, cut a strip of muslin or other fabric the width of the quilt by about 6 inches wide. Fold under the short ends once or twice, and sew. Now, the strip will be narrower than the quilt. Press under the long edges about 1/4 inch, and handstitch to the upper edge of the back of the quilt, centering it.

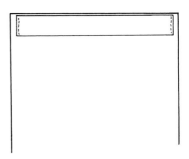

Place two large cup hooks into the wall to support the ends of the dowel. Wooden beads or curtain finials may be glued onto the ends of the dowel to prevent it from slipping off the hooks.

Large quilts hung with a rod pocket should be additionally supported with vertical strips of fabric lightly handstitched to the back of the quilt, running from top to bottom. Have these strips about 2-4 inches wide, and placed about 10 inches apart. Be sure the stitches do not come through to the front of the quilt, but run them through the foundation if possible.

This should be done with any quilt that is weighted with beads and other embellishments, or made of heavy fabrics.

PART TWO
Gallery
of Crazy Quilts

From plain to fancy, useful to decorative, Victorian crazy quilts is a term that covers much territory. Most were made smaller than bed-size and used as decorative throws. These fancy quilts are now sometimes called exhibition, art, or show quilts. Those made of wool, on the other hand, tend to be more plainly embroidered, and were likely to have been used on beds.

I've taken the liberty of some modern interpretations, adapting the crazy quilt to fit many purposes. Refer to previous chapters for construction methods, and embroidery and embellishment details. Any of the quilts can be made the size, colors, embroidery stitches and embellishments of your choice.

Fund-raiser and Commemorative Crazy Quilts

Fund-raiser and commemorative quilts are types that are made by groups rather than individuals. Commemorative quilts can be made to celebrate anniversaries of local importance, such as the founding of a town or city, and raffled off to raise funds. These can be theme quilts, with appliqués and embroideries showing buildings and landmarks that are important to the area's history. Fund-raisers need no theme, although they can be given one.

Fund-raiser quilt made by The Valley Needlers, South Hiram, Maine. 1997.

The Valley Needlers Quilt Guild, members of the Maine State Pine Tree Quilter's Guild, Inc., made a crazy quilt for their annual raffle in 1997. Each block of the quilt was completed by a member of the group. This is a classic crazy quilt in design. Colors, threads and fabrics were chosen by several of the members, and the materials divided sixteen ways for that number of blocks. It took a little over four months with members working on their own and in groups to finish the quilt which was then displayed at the Maine State Quilt Show, and at several fairs and local events. The proceeds from the raffle were used to benefit a local high school.

Theme Crazy Quilts

The antique quilt shown here has a subtly stated theme. "White Rose" is embroidered on one patch, and there is a small embroidered white rose on another. White roses were also important to the previous occupants of the house we live in. There is a rose garden now rescued from thick undergrowth, with all white roses in it, including a once-blooming Alba. All year I await its spectacular blooms and exquisite scent. When it blooms it seems to light up the entire yard, and in moonlight is unforgettable. Something such as this can be both incentive and inspiration for a quilt design.

The "White Rose" quilt is an example of an antique crazy quilt that has a theme. Detail. Photographed at Shiretown Antiques, Alfred, Maine.

A theme can be represented by a central motif, as the Victorian Horse quilt, or by adding appropriate embellishments. The two quilts featured in this Gallery were inspired by antique objects. Here are additional ideas for subjects for theme quilts:

- a favorite vacation spot
- cats, dogs, other animals
- sailing ships and nautical
- flowers, trees, herbs
- sports
- royalty, Egyptian pharaohs, other dignitaries
- fairy tales, mythology, angels

Choose a theme, then find ways to represent it. Appliqué, photo transfer, outline embroidery, words and quotes, painted details, are some ways to get your theme onto a quilt.

The Butterstamp Quilt

Butterstamps and buttermolds feature beautifully carved designs including florals, geometrics, cows, swans, initials, and many others. The hand-carved "folk art" designs were once used to imprint a farm family's homemade butter.

As a theme quilt, this piece displays rubbings of the stamps and molds. The rubbings were done with special crayons designed for fabrics, containing dyes.

The Butterstamp quilt is a theme quilt displaying folk art images; 1994. Collection of Paul Baresel.

A few words were also embroidered onto the quilt patches, including "butter prints," "antiques," "folk art," "Americana," and "Limerick," and the quilt is signed and dated.

Quilt size: 56-1/2 inches wide x 58-3/4 inches long, finished size.

Victorian Horse Quilt

An old fashioned horse toy theme makes this quilt suitable for a collector, a child's room, or decoration in almost any room. A pictorial center such as this one displays a theme grandly, making it the central focus of the quilt. In this type of quilt, the crazy quilting forms a border around the center. An additional, outer border, can also be added. The quilt center can also be used as a central patch on a much larger quilt.

This quilt is available in a pattern, see The Magic Needle under sources.

The Victorian Horse quilt was photographed after the ice storm of January 1998, with an icy garden horse; 1996.

Crazy Quilts for Children

Until recent history, children were expected to learn adult skills including needlework. The small block shown here is a child's piece, on which she learned how to patch, baste and embroider. Even a small fan is included in the center. What better way to learn a variety of stitches, than by crazy quilting!

As an aside, and since we are on the subject of children, it is interesting to note that Queen Victoria did not enjoy her babies. She was always appalled by what she calls in her writings, "that terrible frog-like action" of her nine children when they were infants! However, she did insist that her daughters learn basic needlework skills.

This antique block is likely the work of a child learning to crazy patch and work embroidery stitches. In the center, a fan was attempted. Collection of Rocky Mountain Quilts, York Village, Maine.

The "Cousins" Quilt

The Outline stitched children on this quilt are Kate Greenaway's turn-of-the-century drawings of children. The Kate Greenaway drawings are available as iron-on transfers published by Dover Publications, Inc. See Sources.

The names and dates on this quilt are my son's cousins on the maternal side of the family, courtesy of my Aunt Elda who is researching the family tree. Elda's research has resulted in family reunions (she also publishes a family newsletter!), the only way we get to see each other nowadays. The family is spread out all the way from Oregon to Maine, and some of the names are cousins my son has never met. This was a major impetus to do this quilt, as a reminder that family does indeed exist–somewhere!

Make this quilt the size of your choice. The one shown here is a coverlet for a twin bed. All cotton, it is hand washable. The buttons are optional, ties can be used instead.

Quilt size: 62-1/4 inches wide x 80 inches long, finished size.

The Cousins Quilt is a family heirloom; 1997.

Confetti Crib Quilt

A "quickie" project, this crib-size child's quilt was completely finished in less than a day. The top was made in one piece using the Confetti method. Fabrics used include printed calicos, plain broadcloths in pink and white, and turquoise cotton flannel. It was not embroidered, since the printed fabrics provide sufficient decoration by themselves.

This is a small quilt, intended for crib, stroller, car, and around-the-house use. Baby may choose to adopt it as a carry around blanket! It could also be used as a wall hanging.

To make a similar quilt choose a batting that does not require close quilting. The cotton batting in this quilt allows quilt ties to be about 10 inches apart.

To make a larger size of this type of quilt, the top can be divided into blocks for easier handling.

Quilt size: 26 inches wide x 38 inches long, finished size.

A confetti crib quilt, 1997, is displayed on a rocking horse made by the author's father, Ray Michler (deceased), and a cotton rag rug woven by the author's mother, Doris Michler of Waupaca, Wisconsin.

Miniature Crazy Quilts

Miniatures can be displayed by hanging them the same as larger quilts, or they can be matted and framed. The miniatures here are true minis, not just smaller quilts. They can be very elegant if stitches are finely made, and fabrics and trims carefully chosen.

Miniatures can also be used as "tools." Working in so small a size is an efficient way to try color schemes, embroidery stitches, patch arrangements, and so on

The pieces shown here are color-scheme experiments, of silk fabrics and embroidered with Soie Gobelin, a twisted silk thread that is finer than Soie Perlee. The only embellishments are several tiny embroidered insects on each picture.

These small pieces can be made close to a 1:1 (1 inch = 1 foot) dollhouse scale, although the patches and embroidery will be slightly larger.

Quilt size: 8-1/2 inches square, finished size.

Miniature quilt 1, 1997.

Embroidering insects: ———

These are tiny! Using Soie Gobelin, make them as follows. Two Bullion stitches about 1/2-3/4 inches long, exactly side by side. Padded satin stitches all worked into the same two holes, about 3/8 inch long. Two or three French knots wrapped about 5 times. Two pistil stitches with two wraps each. Two straight or pistil stitches may be added to the back end of the insect's body. Make wings of a second color of thread, each is a Lazy Daisy stitch, make 4 to 6 wings per bug. Legs can be added using the body color, and making two straight stitches for each.

Shape each insect differently by placing the individual parts of the body and the wings at different angles.

Miniature quilt 2, 1997.

Miniature quilt 3, 1997.

Miniature quilt 4, 1997.

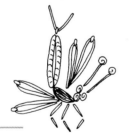

Doll's Quilt ———

Lightweight silk fabrics adapt well to miniature work, because the smallest patches are relatively easy to handle. This 1:1 miniature doll's quilt is mainly a silk quilt, worked on a silk organza foundation, and including a very thin layer of silk batting.

Quilt size: 9 inches wide x 10 inches long, not including a 2 1/4-inch ruffle on three sides.

This 6-inch porcelain baby doll cuddles under her silk crazy quilt. A felt rug will keep her feet warm; 1997.

Patching a miniature quilt: tiny silk patches are laid onto a silk organza foundation.

All-silk Crazy Quilts

Silk quilts can be very elegant, lightweight and warm. The Victorians had sufficient quantities of this fabric, and began to make their scrap quilts out of it instead of cottons. Silks are a common fabric in most of the fancy antique crazy quilts.

All-silk implies the use of all or mostly silk patch fabrics, foundation, trims, and threads. The silk jacket pictured here is 100 percent silk except for the glass seed beads.

Silk cocoon jacket has silk batting and lining, and is beaded to join the layers; 1995.

Silk Jacket

This cocoon-style jacket was made in one piece. Made of all lightweight silks and a thin silk batting, a jacket can retain much of the exceptional drape that silk is known for. Choose a garment style that relies on draping to achieve a fit, and that can be patched all in one piece. Cocoon and short kimono styles are two that will work well.

Detail of a sleeve.

Ladies and Fans Silk Quilt

Pieced fans found on many antique crazy quilts vary in size and shape, from short and wide to long and narrow. They were pieced of fabrics or ribbons. Many needleworkers also added small embroidered, rounded fans with handles, usually indicated simply in Outline stitch. Fans, and double, triple and quadruple rings seem to have been the most common motifs placed on the quilts, even more so than spiderwebs.

This quilt/wall hanging is finished in the style of a bed quilt with the ruffle placed on three sides only.

Size of quilt: 41-1/2 inches wide x 42-1/2 inches long, not including a 3-inch ruffle on three sides.

The Ladies and Fans quilt displays a feminine side of crazy quilting, with cigarette silks of ladies, pieced fans, silk ribbon florals and baskets, ribbonwork, buttons, tassels, and a silk ruffle finish; 1997. The beautiful marbled silk fabrics in this quilt are the work of Ann Shurtleff of Pagosa Springs, Colorado.

Wool and Country-style Crazy Quilts

There may have been many crazy quilts made of wool as a practical alternative to the fancy ones. Many were made with very little fancy embroidery stitching, usually only a single row along patch edges. Embellishment, if any, most often consisted of simple outline stitched shapes.

To press under the seam allowances of patches, use a water-filled spray bottle and a dry iron. Place a press cloth over the wool, then spray lightly, and press. The steam will set the crease. The fabric should be allowed to dry before it is moved.

See the section on wool embroidery in Part 1 of Artful Embellishments. This type of embroidery may be worked on some patch seams, with Victorian stitches on others. Wool embroidery is a very attractive addition to a wool quilt. You can also incorporate pieces of unfinished crewel work, needlepoint, and cross stitch as patches or patch appliqués if there are any lurking in your closets. Ask around for donations if you haven't them. Some folks would rather give them up to a purpose such as this in order to free up closet space (and conscience!).

If you haven't quilted with wool, try a small sample, including embroidery before committing to a large project. The wool fiber behaves differently than other fabrics, and is a material of choice for many who like its pliability, warmth, and texture.

Horses and Roses Wool Quilt

I'm pleased to say that this quilt is unfinished! Refusing to buy into a modern notion that everything need be done quickly, I find it very de-stressing to pick up something that is "in progress" and just stitch away.

The idea of things being done quickly I think is ironic. We have available so many appliances, from the kitchen to the sewing room, that speedily do what once took lots of time and human energy. I think this paraphernalia gives the impression that all things in life should also be so quick and easy. The irony is that they were originally intended to free up our time, allowing more time for crazy quilting and other fun things!

This quilt is half finished. It is to be a coverlet for a queen size bed, and there will be 6 additional blocks. The wool embroidery is a winter thing to do, leaving the cross stitch and needlepoint pieces to be done in summer when wool is too heavy to work on.

Quilt size: 73 inches wide x 93 inches long, finished size not including the lace edging.

Horses and Roses. Unfinished. The cross stitch horses are the original works of the author.

The Horses and Roses quilt draped, with the Folk Hearts hanging. Both are at home in a country-style setting.

Art Crazy Quilts

The quilting movement of recent years has given rise to quiltmaking at all levels, some of it better classified as textile arts. This is both exciting and encouraging to those who enjoy the creativity. These quilts are characterized by original patching or piecing that follows no previous conventions, some of them embellished and/or embroidered. Art quilts are a "follow your heart or artistic conscience" type of quilting, a description that easily includes most crazy quilts. Pushing the boundaries of crazy quilting can elevate the artistry involved.

To challenge yourself, try the suggestion given in the chapter on using colors. Choose some colors that make you say "yuck." This is what I did in the Piano Shawl quilt, the light mossy greens and lime greens are colors I did not gravitate to. In addition, greens as a focal color are fairly new to my color agenda which previously included many reds and purples. After making this quilt, I find it easier and more natural to include greens of many shades in my projects.

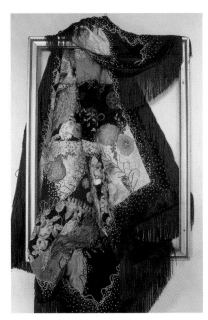

The Piano Shawl shown "framed" demonstrates the draping potential of crazy quilts if they are made with materials that allow them to do so.

The Piano Shawl

Silks can be substituted for the rayon fabrics. There are many French Knots in this quilt, my favorite stitch. Drape this quilt over a grand piano, or wear it to a party!
This quilt is made of rayon challis and other fabrics, on a foundation of cotton batiste. Quilt size: 42 inches square, finished size, not including a 4-inch fringe.

Detail of the Piano Shawl.

The Piano Shawl; 1996.

Landscape hanging; 1998.

Memory Quilts

The Victorian version of a memory quilt was a mourning quilt, made after a loved one passed on. Mourning crazy quilts tend to be dark (made mostly of black fabrics), somber, and dismal-looking. The memories evoked by these would be more significant of the grief of the mourner, rather than a celebration of the person now gone.

Now, fortunately, we are more likely to celebrate the happy memories, the good thoughts, the memorable moments. A quilt that documents a person's lifetime, a specific life event, or a part of one's life qualifies as a memory piece.

Detail of a Victorian mourning quilt. Collection of Rocky Mountain Quilts, York Village, Maine.

The Victorian Quilt

This quilt is a collection of much that I've done as a writer and designer for the business, The Magic Needle of Limerick, Maine during its 12 or so years of existence. Some of the embroideries are "trial" things, design starts, and ideas worked out "in the cloth." My first impression of this quilt is that it is a true scrap-bag piece, but 20 years from now I'll be looking at with nostalgia.
Quilt size: 54 inches wide x 52 inches long, finished size.

A Shadowbox Piece

Photographs printed on fabric are an obvious way to remember people, places and things, and they are often used in memory quilts of many types. When I think of my grandmother gone for several years now, I remember more of what she left behind–crocheted laces, memories of her corn relish and love of gardening, a black bead necklace –than her visual image.

In this piece, velveteen patches were stenciled with a moon, a tree, hollyhock, and a fern, and then embroidered.

Shadowbox, a memory piece, 1998. This shadowbox was made out of an antique picture frame.

Victorian Quilt; 1994. The marbled silk fabrics in this quilt are by Ann Shurtleff of Pagosa Springs, Colorado.

The Meanings of Flowers

The Victorians attached great importance to meanings given to flowers. These were used as a communication device by young lovers; in bouquets, and valentines, for example. Flowers hold meanings for love, death, general and religious purposes. In addition, herbs, trees and vegetables were given meanings.

Those listed here are excerpted from two books: The Bouquet: Containing The Poetry and Language of Flowers, by a Lady, published by Benjamin B. Mussey, Boston, 1846. This is a charming small book with gold edged pages, and a poem for each flower. The other is a hefty tome, titled Woman's World, A Complete Guide to Perfect Womanhood, by Mary Alice Sullivan, published by Monarch Book Co., Philadelphia, PA, 1894.

Use the flowers individually or in bouquets to combine meanings. Create secret "messages" on a crazy quilt! Or, choose a flower because of its meaning and make a theme quilt around the idea. Consult with flower encyclopedias and illustrated gardening catalogs for pictures of the flowers.

Flower	Meaning
Acacia, yellow	Concealed love
Aconite (Wolfsbane)	Misanthropy
Almond (Flowering)	Hope
Aloe	Religious superstition
Alyssum (Sweet)	Worth beyond beauty
Amaranth, Globe	Unchangeable, unfading love
Amaryllis	Pride, timidity, splendid beauty
Anemone	Anticipation
Angelica	Inspiration
Apple	Temptation
Arbor Vitae	Unchanging friendship, live for me
Auricula, scarlet	Wealth is not happiness
Bachelor's Button	I with the morning's love have oft made sport
Balm	Sympathy
Balsamine	Impatience
Basil	Hatred
Bay Leaf	I change but in dying
Belladonna	Silence
Betony	Surprise
Bluebell	Constancy
Borage	Bluntness
Box	Stoicism
Cabbage	Profit
Cactus	Warmth
Camellia, white	Perfect loveliness
Candytuft	Indifference
Canterbury Bell	Acknowledgment
Chamomile	Energy in adversity
China Aster	Variety is charming
Chrysanthemum, red	I love you
Clematis	Mental beauty
Cloves	Dignity
Columbine	I cannot give thee up
Coreopsis	Love at first sight
Corn	Riches
Cowslip	Pensiveness, winning grace
Crocus	Cheerfulness
Currant	Thy frown will kill me
Daffodil	Regard
Daisy	Beauty and innocence
Damask Rose	Brilliant complexion
Dandelion	Coquetry
Dew Plant	Serenade
Dogwood	Durability
Eglantine	I wound to heal
Endive	Frugality
Eupatorium	Delay
Everlasting	Always remembered
Fennel	Strength
Fern	Fascination
Flax	Domestic industry
Flowering Reed	Confidence in Heaven
Forget-me-not	True love
Foxglove	Insincerity
Geranium, Oak	True friendship
Geranium, Rose	Preference
Gilly Flower	Bonds of affection
Goldenrod	Precaution
Grass	Submission
Harebell	Grief
Hawthorne	Hope
Heath	Solitude is sometimes best society
Heliotrope	Devotion, faithfulness
Hibiscus	Delicate beauty
Hollyhock	Ambition
Honey Flower	My love is sweet and secret
Houstonia	Contentment
Hyacinth	Sport, game, play
Hydrangea	Heartlessness
Hyssop	Cleanliness
Ice Plant	Your looks freeze me
Iris	I have a message for you
Ivy	Wedded love
Jacob's Ladder	Come down to me
Japan Rose	Beauty is your only attraction
Jasmine, white	Amiability
Jonquil	I desire a return of affection
Laburnum	Pensive beauty
Lady's Slipper	Win me and wear me
Larkspur	Fickleness
Laurel	Glory
Laurustinus	I die if neglected
Lily, white	Purity and sweetness
Lily of the Valley	Delicate simplicity
Locust	Affection beyond the grave
Lotus	Eloquence
Love-in-a-mist	You puzzle me
Love Lies Bleeding	Hopeless, not heartless
Magnolia	Love of nature
Mallow	Mildness
Marigold, French	Jealousy
Meadowsweet	Uselessness
Mignonette	Your qualities surpass your loveliness
Mimosa	Sensitiveness
Mint	Virtue
Mistletoe	I surmount all difficulties
Monkshood	Chivalry
Morning Glory	Affectation
Myrtle	Love in absence
Narcissus, Poet's	Self-love, egotism
Nasturtium	Patriotism
Nightshade	Truth
Oats	Music
Oleander	Beware
Orange Blossom	Your purity equals your loveliness
Ox Eye	Patience
Parsley	Feasting, entertainment
Pansy	Tender and pleasant thoughts
Passion Flower	Religious fervor
Pasque Flower	You have no claims
Pea, Everlasting	Wilt thou go with me?
Pea, Sweet	Departure
Peach Blossom	I am your captive
Peony	Shame, bashfulness
Periwinkle, blue	Sweet remembrance
Phlox	Our souls are united
Poppy, red	Forgetfulness, or consolation
Poppy, white	Sleep of the heart
Primrose	Early youth
Primrose, Evening	Inconstancy
Queen's Rocket	You are the queen of coquettes
Quince	Temptation
Ranunculus	You are radiant with charms
Rhododendron	Danger, beware
Rose	Love
Rose, bridal	Happy love
Rose, moss	Superior merit
Rosemary	Remembrance
Rue	Disdain
Sage	Domestic virtues
Shamrock	Light-heartedness
Speedwell	Fidelity
Spiderwort	Esteem, not love
Star of Bethlehem	Light of our path
St. John's Wort	Animosity
Stock	Lasting beauty
Sunflower, dwarf	Your devout admirer
Syringa	Memory
Tansy	I declare war against you
Tuberose	Dangerous pleasures
Tulip, red	A declaration of love
Verbena	Sensibility
Veronica	Fidelity
Violet	Modesty
Wallflower	Fidelity in misfortune
Weeping Willow	Mourning
Witch Hazel	A spell
Woodbine	Fraternal love
Wormwood	Absence
Yarrow	Thou alone must care
Yew	Sorrow
Zinnia	Thoughts of absent friends

Selected Bibliography

Bond, Dorothy. *Crazy Quilt Stitches.* self published: 1981.

Brandt, Janet Carija. *Wow! Wool-on-Wool Folk Art Quilts.* That Patchwork Place, 1995.

Burchell, S.C, and The Editors of Time-Life Books. *Age of Progress.* NY: Time-Life Books, 1966.

Caulfield, S.F.A., Saward, Blanche C. *Encyclopedia of Victorian Needlework (Dictionary of Needlework)*, Vols. 1 & 2. NY: Dover Publications, 1972. Unabridged republication of the second edition (1887) of the work originally published by A.W. Cowan, London in 1882 under the title *The Dictionary of Needlework: An Encyclopedia of Artistic, Plain, and Fancy Needlework.*

Chijiwa, Hideaki, *Color Harmony: A Guide to Creative Color Combinations.* MA: Rockport Publishers, 1987.

Christopher, Barbara. *Traditional Chinese Designs: Iron-on Transfer Patterns.* NY: Dover Publications, Inc., 1987.

Coats, J&P, Ltd. *The Anchor Manual of Needlework.* Interweave Press, 1990.

Conroy, Mary. *The Complete Book of Crazy Patchwork: A Step-by-Step Guide to Crazy Patchwork Projects.* NY: Sterling Publishing Co., Inc., 1985.

Fanning, Robbie and Tony. *The Complete Book of Machine Embroidery.* Chilton Book Company, 1986.

Gardner, Pat Long. *Handkerchief Quilts.* Virginia: EPM, 1993.

Glazier, Richard. *Historic Textile Fabrics.* Great Britain, 1923.

Hasler, Julie S. Kate Greenaway *Iron-on Transfer Patterns.* NY: Dover Publications, Inc., 1990.

Haywood, Dixie. *Crazy Quilt Patchwork: A Quick and Easy Approach with 19 Projects.* NY: Dover Publications, Inc., 1986.

Hibbert, Christopher. *Queen Victoria in Her Letters and Journals, A Selection.* NY: Viking, 1985.

Horton, Laurel, editor. *Quiltmaking in America, Beyond the Myths.* Nashville, TN: Rutledge Hill Press, 1994.

Hulbert, Anne. *Folk Art Quilts: 20 Unique Designs from the American Museum in Britain.* London, England: Collins & Brown, Ltd., 1996.

Hubert, Carol. *An Introduction to Wool Embroidery.* Australia: Kangaroo Press, 1991.

Jarratt, Maisie. *French Embroidery Beading: How to Bead.* Australia: Kangaroo Press, 1991.

Kolander, Cheryl. *A Silkworker's Notebook.* Loveland, CO: Interweave Press, Inc. Revised edition, 1985.

Laury, Jean Ray. *Imagery on Fabric.* CA: C&T Publishing, 1992.

MacColl, Gail, Wallace, Carol McD. *To Marry an English Lord.* NY: Workman Publishing, 1989.

Maisel Ph.D., Eric. *Fearless Creating: A Step-by-Step Guide to Starting and Completing your Work of Art.* NY: Tarcher/Putnam, 1995.

McMorris, Penny. *Crazy Quilts.* E.P. Dutton, 1984.

Michler, J. Marsha. *Ribbon Embroidery, with 178 Iron-on Transfers.* Mineola, NY: Dover Publications, Inc., 1997.

Montano, Judith B. *The Handbook of Crazy Quilting.* C&T Publishing, 1986.

- *Crazy Quilt Odyssey.* C&T Publishing, 1991.

Nichols, Marion. *Encyclopedia of Embroidery Stitches, Including Crewel.* NY: Dover Publications, Inc., 1974.

Nylander, Jane C. *Fabrics for Historic Buildings.* Washington, DC: The Preservation Press, 1983.

Parker, Freda. *Victorian Embroidery.* NY: Crescent Books, 1991.

Rankin, Chris. *Splendid Silk Ribbon Embroidery.* NY: Sterling Publishing Co., Inc., 1996.

Ruhling, Nancy and Freeman, John Crosby. *The Illustrated Encyclopedia of Victoriana, A Comprehensive Guide to the Designs, Customs, and Inventions of the Victorian Era.* Philadelphia PA, 1994.

Ryan, Mildred Graves. *The Complete Encyclopedia of Stitchery.* NY: Doubleday & Co., Inc., 1979.

Turpin-Delport, Lesley. *Satin and Silk Ribbon Embroidery.* South Africa: Triple T Publishing, 1993.

Walton, Perry. *The Story of Textiles.* 1925.

Weintraub, Stanley. *Victoria.* NY: Dutton, 1987.

Welch, Nancy. *Tassels: the Fanciful Embellishment.* Asheville, NC: Lark Books, 1992.

Wells, Jean. *Memorabilia Quilting.* CA: C&T Publishing, 1992.

Wilson, Erica. *Erica Wilson's Embroidery Book.* NY: Charles Scribner's Sons, 1973.

Wingate, Isabel B., and Mohler, *June F. Textile Fabrics and their Selection*, 8th Ed.

Sources

The following is a selected listing of sources of supplies for crazy quilting and other needle arts:

Retail Mail Order Sources

Crazy quilt patterns, materials packages for crazy quilting:
The Magic Needle
RR 2, Box 172
Limerick, ME 04048
email: jmmichlr@gwi.net
Send $2.00 for a catalog.

Original paintings on silk patches:
The Willow Shop
RR2 Box 834
Limerick, ME 04048
Write for information.

Needlework supplies, beads, club:
Evening Star Designs
69 Coolidge Ave.
Haverhill, MA 01832
Send $3.00 for a catalog.

Vintage kimono fabrics for quilt patches:
Katie's Vintage Kimono
P.O. Box 1813
Belfair, WA 98528
360-275-2815
email: kendrick@hctc.com
website:
http://www.hctc.com/~kendrick

Antique fabrics and quilts, high quality reproduction fabrics, conservation and restoration supplies. "The Crazy Quilt Society," annual conference and newsletter:
The Kirk Collection
1513 Military Ave.
Omaha, NE 68111
1-800-398-2542
email: KirkColl@aol.com
website: http://www.kirkcollection.com
Needlework supplies:

Very Victorian Notions
P.O. Box 18-M
Denver, CO 80218-0170
Send $3.00 for a catalog.

Victorian needlework supplies, books:
Lacis
3163 Adeline St.
Berkeley, CA 94703
510-843-7178
email: staff@lacis.com
website: www.lacis.com

"The Catalog of Craft Books, Kits & Gifts"
Lark Books
50 College St.
Asheville, NC 28801

Iron-on transfers for embroidery, crochet edgings patterns:
Dover Publications, Inc.
31 East 2nd St.
Mineola, NY 11501-3582
Request their catalog of needlework books.

Glass seed beads:
Shipwreck Beads
2727 Westmoor Ct. SW
Olympia, WA 98502
www.shipwreck.com
email: beads@shipwreck.com

Silk fabrics:
Thai Silks!
252 State St.
Los Altos, CA 94022

Silk fabrics and dyes:
Rupert, Gibbon & Spider
P.O. Box 425
Healdsburg, CA 95448

Natural dyes, kits, things to dye:
Color Trends
5129 Ballard Ave. NW
Seattle, WA 98107
email: earthues@aol.com

Catalog of Sewing & Craft Supplies:
Home Sew
P.O. Box 4099
Bethlehem, PA 18018-0099
Customer service: 610-867-9717

Antique quilts including crazy quilts for sale, antique laces, cigarette silks and felts:
Rocky Mountain Quilts
130 York Street
York Village, ME 03909

Restoration of quilts:
3847 Alt. 6 & 24
Palisade, CO 81526

Email mailing lists for quilting, chat rooms, catalogs, clubs:
website: http://www.quiltropolis.com/
email: info@quiltropolis.com
804-730-0672

Wholesale Sources

Write or call these businesses to be referred to the nearest retailer of a mail-order source.

Natural-dyed linen fabrics, linen threads, silk ribbons:
Green Mountain Hand Dyed Linens
P.O. Box 206
North Clarendon, VT 05759-0206
web site: http://www. sover.net/~mitlfrah/users.html

Impressions®, Wildflowers®, Waterlilies® hand-dyed threads:
The Caron Collection
55 Old South Rd.
Stratford, CT 06497
www.caron-net.com
email: mail@caron-net.com

Hand-dyed cotton and wool threads:
Needle Necessities, Inc.
14746 N.E. 95th St.
Redmond, WA 98052

Soie Perlee, Soie Gobelins, Soie D'Alger, Silk Serica® threads, metallic threads, restoration gauze, fine cotton thread:
Kreinik Customer Service Dept.
3106 Timanus Lane, Suite 101
Baltimore, MD 21244
800-537-2166
http://www.kreinik.com
email: kreinik@kreinik.com

Instant-setting silk dye kits, supplies, silk ribbons:
Things Japanese
9805 N.E. 116th St., Suite 7160
Kirkland, WA 98034-2287

Silk ribbons, trims:
Janice Naibert
16590 Emory Lane
Rockville, MD 20853

Punchneedles and supplies:
Clarke's Oh Sew Easy Needle, Inc.
2004 Main St., Suite 210
Forest Grove, OR 97116

Silk and other ribbons for resale and for kitmakers:
Ribbon Connections, Inc.
969 Industrial Rd., Suite E
San Carlos, CA 94070

Silk rovings that can be pulled apart and used for batting inside silk quilts. Linen and other yarns:
Louet Sales, Inc.
Box 267
Ogdensburg, NY 13669
www.cybertap.com/louet/
email: louet@cybertap.com

Glass seed beads, heart beads, linen fabrics:
Wichelt Imports, Inc.
N162 Hwy 35
Stoddard, WI 54658
website: www.wichelt.com

Swiss embroidered edgings, cotton laces, cotton satin fabric:
Capitol Imports, Inc.
P.O. Box 13002
Tallahassee, FL 32317
904-385-4665

Magazines and Organizations

Needlework history and projects:
Piecework Magazine
Interweave Press
201 East Fourth St.
Loveland, CO 80537-5655
website: http://www.interweave.com

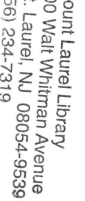

Mount Laurel Library
100 Walt Whitman Avenue
Mt. Laurel, NJ 08054-9539
(856) 234-7319

Embroidery designs, patterns, instructions:
Inspirations Magazine
Country Bumpkin
76a Kensington Road, Rose Park
South Australia 5067
(also available in the U.S. from many retailers)
An organization with many local chapters, correspondence courses, magazine: "Needle Arts":
The Embroiderer's Guild of America, Inc.
335 West Broadway, Suite 100
Louisville, KY 40202

Create beautiful and unique quilts with the help of these books

See what projects are awaiting your creative touch

Beaded Adornment
by Jeanette Shanigan
Create a treasured collection of necklace and earring sets that are sure to astound and make a statement. Author Jeanette Shanigan shares six beadwork techniques to create twenty-three projects. You need not be an experienced artist because the simple, fully photographed instructions cover projects for all levels of beadworkers.

Softcover • 8-1/4 x 10-7/8
128 pages • 100 Line Drawings
150 color photos
BEAD • $19.95

Exotic Beads
by Sara Withers
Basic techniques and clearly annotated color photos help you create 45 distinctive designs with readily available materials and beads. The only book to fully explore ethnic influences in beadwork, it's inspiring for beginners and those more experienced.

Softcover • 8-1/4 x 10-7/8
128 pages color throughout
EXBE • $19.95

Beautiful Beads
by Alexandra Kidd
More than 50 projects await your creative touch! How-tos and inspirational ideas feature basic and advanced techniques with glass, wood, plastic, crystal, and polymer clay beads. Instructions for jewelry, accessories, home decor accents, more.

Softcover • 8-1/4 x 10-7/8 • 128 pages color throughout
BEBE • $19.95

The Irresistible Bead Designing and Creating Exquisite
Beadwork Jewelry
by Linda Fry Kenzle
Capture the allure of beads while taking beadwork jewelry into the next century. Twenty multi-faceted projects illustrate techniques such as wire work, molding polymer clay, stringing beads and weaving beads for brooches, bags, necklaces, earrings and more.

Softcover • 8-1/4 x 10-7/8
128 pages color throughout
IRBE • $19.95

The Techniques Of Japanese Embroidery
by Shuji Tamura
Learn to create beautiful traditional Japanese embroideries using detailed illustrations and diagrams for more than 50 stitching techniques. Techniques and designs range from flowers, trees, and birds to more abstract works.

Softcover • 8-3/8 x 10-7/8
144 pages • 150 illustrations
90 color photos
TJE • $23.95

Glorious Ribbons
by Christine Kingdom
Weave it. Pleat it. Fold it. Then try embroidery and applique - all with ribbon. Bows, baskets, roses, garlands and 50 other projects provide you with hours of crafting pleasure and fill your home with affordable accents and exquisitely personal touches.

Softcover • 8-1/4 x 10-7/8
128 pages color throughout
GLRI • $19.95